No Blood No Money

How to Make It, Keep It, and Pass It On To Your Loved Ones

No BLOOD No MONEY

How to Make It, Keep It, and
Pass It On To Your Loved Ones

Second Edition

BY RICHARD L. RUBINO, J.D. &
SAMUEL J. LIANG

www.AcanthusPublishing.com

Published by Acanthus Publishing,
a division of The Ictus Group, LLC
343 Commercial Street
Unit 214, Union Wharf
Boston, MA 02109

Library of Congress Cataloging-in-Publication Data
(Provided by The Donohue Group, Inc.)

Rubino, Richard L.
    No blood, no money : how to make it, keep it, and
    pass it on to your loved ones / by Richard L. Rubino and
    Samuel J. Liang.--2nd ed.
    p. : charts ; cm.
    ISBN-13: 978-1-933631-42-4
    ISBN-10: 1-933631-42-2

    1. Finance, Personal. 2. Estate planning.
    3. Retirement--Planning. 4. Saving and investment.
    I. Liang, Samuel J. II. Title.

    HG179.R83 2006
    332.024/016

Printed in the United States of America
10 9 8 7 6 5 4 3 2 1

To my mother, Connie, and Sam's parents,
Johnny and Florence.

Without the wisdom they so lovingly passed on to us,
this book would never have been written.

Thank You's

Both Sam and I would like to thank all who have helped to contribute to this book, including: Attorney Robert Weinstein, Attorney Neil Schauer, and our many clients (many of whom have become friends) who have reinforced the "no blood, no money" philosophy handed down to us by our families.

We also want to give special thanks to our wives, Winnie and Eileen, for putting up with us and encouraging us in our business.

Table of Contents

Foreword

Our practice started in 1989 when Sam and I first began working together. Sam is 20 years younger than me, so between his youthful energy and sharp financial mind and my "gray" hair experience and legal background, we became a dynamic team.

As the years have passed, we have became more and more familiar with each other's families. Sam, born in Hong Kong, came to this country in 1974 with his parents. He was the youngest of five children and the only boy — which meant he was treated like a king. His mom and dad had "old world" values that translated into family coming first.

I was born in Brooklyn, New York and was the middle child of three. I grew up as a Brooklyn Dodgers fan, and when they went to the West Coast I was a boy without a team. After attending law school in Boston, I quickly became a Red Sox fan — they were very similar to the Brooklyn Dodgers.

My dad, Anthony, was born in New York, New York and started working when he was 12 years old. He became a successful clothing designer in New York City. He passed away 25 years ago at the age of 64. My dad taught me how to be a successful businessman — be truthful and provide exceptional service.

My mom, Connie, was born in Naples, Italy and came to this country when she was four years old. She was one of five children, and grew up in Brooklyn during the Depression. Again, family values dominated her upbringing. Whenever anyone in the family got sick, all would gather and take care of that person. The thought of having someone go into a nursing home would never enter anyone's mind.

While I was going to college in New York (St. John's University) I lived at home, and every day after classes I would come home and talk to my mother about a myriad of things. I also learned how to cook, because all our conversations took place in the kitchen.

Her thoughts and philosophies have guided me throughout my life, especially her saying, "having good friends is great but there is nothing better than having a close family." When I was young, I would find myself disagreeing with my mom, only to discover years later that she was right. The term "no blood, no money" came from her. I don't remember whether or not she actually said it, or it if was just her philosophy that came through in our many discussions, but it has always been an important concept to her.

This book is intended to be a resource guide for people ages 55 and up. I have learned that people of these particular generations think along the same lines as my mother, who is 89 years old and widowed. Her "no blood, no money" philosophy is simple — if you aren't in the bloodline, you don't get anything. Although I've been married to my wife, Winnie, for over 32 years, she isn't part of my mother's estate plan. But my mother trusted Winnie enough to be the trustee of our children's potential inheritance when they were younger, so Winnie has become "blood" in a sense!

The people of my mother's generation are savers — they don't want for anything, nor do they waste anything. For example, my mother can't understand why anyone would buy rubber bands. You get rubber bands by saving them, just like bags, pencils, paperclips, sugar packets, etc. There are drawers in her home full of "free stuff."

People of the generations that have followed are much different. They now throw out the free rubber bands, pencils, paperclips, etc. and go to one of the many office supply mega-stores to buy new ones.

The generations also differ greatly in their attitudes toward divorce: in my mother's generation, divorce was taboo, and therefore rare. Now divorce is much more common, which can create much more complicated legal situations for estate planning.

The inability of the people of my mom's generation to spend money gives rise to a great deal of wealth to be transferred to the next generation. It is not uncommon for an individual who was a blue-collar worker to have amassed an estate (real estate and liquid assets) in excess of $1 million. If you have two children, each gets $500,000 when you die — how do you keep that money in the bloodline and divorce-proof the inheritance?

After being partners with Sam for 14 plus years, we have discovered that even though his parents were born in Hong Kong, and my mom was born in Italy, the estate plan mantra of "no blood, no money" is a universal one.

Of course, just as Winnie and I have become one family and Sam and Eileen have become one family, bloodlines do mix. In reality, "no blood, no money" is about family and those you love and care about. How to make sure your loved ones receive all you have worked hard for and saved for is really what this book is all about.

Throughout this book, Sam and I will sprinkle in our respective parents' ways of thinking. Their way is really only one way — the family way.

Part I

Building Wealth: How to Make It & Where To Put It

Chapter 1

I Can't Believe I'm a Millionaire —
But a Million's Not Worth
What it Used to Be

RICH REMARKS:

When I tell my mom she's a millionaire she can't believe it. At 89 years old she still clips coupons and checks every grocery store receipt to make sure she isn't being overcharged. She grew up during the Depression and values every dollar.

Most self-made individuals did it the same way: spend some but make sure you save some.

My mom is still saving for her "old age" at 89 years old. It has become a habit — a good habit.

She would like to make sure that her assets will provide her a comfortable lifestyle and stay in the "bloodline" when she departs this world.

Congratulations. You're a millionaire and you didn't even know it. That's because you've probably been sitting on some property — a house, a condo, or land — that has skyrocketed in value since you purchased it 5, 10, 25, or 50 years ago. And, if you're like other Americans, you've probably been pretty savvy with your finances: making smart investments; saving your money in bank accounts, CDs, and bonds; shopping for bargains. Earning more. Spending less.

A million dollars was once considered a lot of money. In 1949, an average baseball player was lucky to make $7,000 a year before taxes. Today, the average baseball player makes close to $2 million a year.

Believe it or not, a million dollars isn't worth very much today. That's partly because there are so many millionaires in the world — in fact, anyone who owns a house, a bank account, and an insurance policy in any of the major cities across the country is probably close to being a millionaire. What does this mean? Overall, that as time goes by, the cost of things such as property, food, clothes, and medicine has gone up. You pay more. You get less.

Being "just a millionaire" isn't so bad. In fact, in some parts of the country, a million dollars will get you a long way. The same $300,000 home you buy in Boston may only cost you $90,000 in Arizona. How far your money will take you depends on what you plan to do with the amount you already have and whether or not you'll be able to get more as time goes by.

How Much Money Do I Need To Last the Rest of My Life?

Well, that depends on the following factors:

1) The age at which you plan to retire

People today treat retirement like another stage of life. Some people retire early, in their 50s or 60s, some work well into their 80s. Baby Boomers, in general, are expected to retire at an earlier age than previous generations.

If you retire before the age of 65, you're going to have to save more money because you'll stop working sooner. And you'll probably live a lot longer than your grandparents or even your parents did. You're also going to have to plan ahead for your health insurance because Medicare doesn't start until age 65.

Begin estimating what you have in your retirement savings. It's never too late to start stashing money away into a 401(k) or IRA, though it's always better to start as soon as possible. If you're over 50, many plans have "catch-up" options that allow you to make larger annual contributions to your retirement savings.

When planning for retirement, you also want to evaluate potential future expenses. For example, if you have kids, remember that college costs could heavily impact your ability to save. Plan ahead and be prepared.

2) How much you can expect to draw as income from Social Security, retirement plans, and other investments

There are still ways to draw income, even after you stop working. For most retired people this income comes in three forms: Social Security, retirement plans, and investments.

The amount you get from Social Security during retirement is determined by your highest income earned in 35 years. To get the full benefit of this Social Security income, you need to retire at the age of 65. If you retire between the ages of 62 and 65, you get a reduced benefit that will impact the amount you receive for the remainder of your life.

How much you'll need to withdraw from individual or employer-provided retirement accounts to supplement Social Security depends on when you begin taking Social Security. For example, if you retire at 63, you'll have to draw more from your other plans to make up for lost benefits. Another thing to consider about Social Security is the fact that the ratio of workers to beneficiaries is decreasing, which means there's no guarantee Social Security income will remain at current levels. In fact, by the time you retire, there may be no Social Security at all.

Retired people also receive income through retirement plans. These plans include pensions, annuity accounts, 401(k)s, 403(b)s, traditional IRAs, and Roth IRAs. Factoring the amount of money you'll need to set aside in these plans can be complicated, so consult a financial adviser.

Social Security Reform

Social Security was created during the Depression of the 1930s to give the elderly and disabled a decent standard of living. At the time, there were about 40 workers per beneficiary. Today, there are only 3.5 workers per beneficiary, and with 77 million Baby Boomers starting to retire later in this decade, the number of contributing workers will become increasingly disproportionate. Although Social Security currently takes in more than it pays out in benefits, that situation is projected to change by 2018, when the system will start to run big deficits. In addition to fiscal problems, Social Security provides no actual property rights, so an individual could work 30 years, die before reaching age 65, and never collect any of his contributions. As we go to print, President Bush is proposing to allow younger workers to invest a portion of their Social Security taxes in private accounts similar to an IRA or 401(k). This proposal is certain to be at the center of debate in Washington and may alleviate some of the problems with the current system. However, private accounts will require workers to become more educated about their finances. In addition, private accounts will have to be paid for and may require cuts in current benefit levels and/or increases in the payroll tax. Stay tuned…

In addition to Social Security and retirement plans, additional income for retirement can also come from investments in businesses, real estate, or annuities, as well as any inheritance or supplemental income you receive from family members or loved ones.

3) How much your medical bills will increase over the years

When planning for the future, it's important to consider your health and the health of your spouse. Remember that you're likely to have more health problems as you age, which means you'll need money to cover the costs of hospital care, doctors' visits, medication, and other associated health expenses.

Medicare Prescription Drug Coverage

In December 2003, Congress passed a new drug benefit as part of the Medicare program (Part D) to help seniors pay for prescriptions. The drug benefit begins January 2006 and is intended primarily to provide for seniors with high or "catastrophic" drug costs and no existing coverage. It isn't designed as a replacement for plans offered to retirees by their former employer(s). As a result, the Medicare drug benefit is not as generous as many retirement plans and has built-in coverage gaps. The standard benefit will work as follows:

1. Seniors will pay a premium of about $35/month.
2. $250 deductible – The first $250/year in drug costs must be paid by seniors before coverage kicks in (no coverage for first $250).
3. The Medicare plan will pay 25% of drug costs between $250 and $2,250/year (seniors are responsible for the remaining 75%).
4. Seniors must pay all of their drug costs between $2,250 and $5,100/year (no coverage in this range). This $2,850 coverage gap has been dubbed the "hole in the doughnut."
5. For prescription drug expenses greater than $5,100/year, the Medicare plan will pay 95% (seniors are responsible for the remaining 5%). This "catastrophic" coverage is the most generous provision in the new drug benefit.

As you can see, the new Medicare drug benefit is complex and provides the most coverage to those seniors with "catastrophic" drug costs (more than $5,100/year). Below $5,100, seniors will be responsible for the bulk — if not all — of their own drug costs. In addition, there are concerns about whether the Medicare drug plan will be financially viable in the future. Therefore, it's essential to weigh your options carefully and consult with your financial advisor to make sure you have adequate coverage.

While Medicare provides government-funded health insurance for elderly people, it doesn't start until age 65. If you or your spouse retire before the age of 65, you're going to need some other kind of private health insurance to fill the gap. If you're 65 and your spouse is 62, Medicare will only cover you.

Currently, Medicare doesn't cover the cost of long-term care, so these costs have to factor into your plan for saving. (See Chapter 11)

4) Whether you or your partner are protected by long-term care insurance

If you have a chronic illness, you have to pay for your own nursing home costs. Medicaid, a means-tested government program, provides money for long-term care, but you can't qualify for it until you spend down your assets to a certain amount. Long-term care insurance, however, will protect assets and preserve your estate for your loved ones. The premiums for this insurance usually cost less if you purchase it earlier, so it's good to take advantage of it before you retire.

5) Whether you can stay financially afloat if your partner dies

Your Social Security and pension income could decline if your spouse dies because the benefit you receive is generally factored toward the couple. There are various types of life insurance that can make up for this lost income. Life insurance can also provide replacement income to cover the expenses of children and other financial dependents.

6) How much you want to leave your family and loved ones

Ten years into retirement you don't want to start spending the money you set aside for your grandkids' education or to help pay off your children's mortgages. You'd like to have something set aside for them — some kind of wealth, whether it's money, stocks, or property — that can be passed easily through the bloodline.

Start thinking about your estate plan now and remember to keep it up to date as changes happen in your family. Take into account such things as estate taxes and probate costs and use wealth preservation techniques such as trusts. Explore the use of these planning tools with an attorney. Find investments that allow you to earn interest while protecting any principal you're saving for your heirs. Your financial advisor can help you identify alternatives that are appropriate for your situation.

Chapter 2

Where Can I Put My Money?
The Three Types of Investments

SAM COMMENTS:

My parents spent most of their lives in Hong Kong and things there are a little different. Their idea of an aggressive investment is a five-year bank CD, which is OK when interest rates are high, but that doesn't produce enough income for them in a low interest rate environment. Over the years I've had my parents transfer some of their accounts to fixed annuities, which provide them with the income they need while maintaining their principal. Their world expanded when they came to this country — both in terms of geography and investment diversity.

L et's assume you don't want to keep the money you're setting aside for financial independence, and your family down the road, under a mattress. Where can you put it?

There are basically three types of investments in which you can put your money: tangible property, intangible property, and real estate property. Each type of property has its own benefits and disadvantages in advancing and securing wealth.

TANGIBLE PROPERTY INVESTMENTS

Tangible property is basically anything you can touch — jewelry, furniture, cars, antiques, stamps, art, household goods, baseball cards, etc. People amass tangible property throughout their lives. Some of it's valuable, some of it's junk, and some of it has sentimental value that goes beyond market price.

Depending on the situation, tangible property can lose or acquire value over time. For example, 10 years ago, you may have bought an antique desk at a flea market that has now doubled in value, but the car you bought 10 years ago (unless it's a collector's item) most likely has decreased in value. Some tangible property appreciates, or increases in value, some doesn't. Appreciation and depreciation depend on many factors, including how rare the item is and how many people there are in the world willing to buy it from you.

As a general rule, it isn't good to base your financial independence on tangible property. The value of collectibles and antiques isn't constant. They change frequently depending on demand and the condition of the item. Tangible property is also a lot more difficult to liquidate, or convert to ready cash when you need it. You have to find a buyer for your item. This could take awhile and in the end you might not get the price you want for it.

Tangible property may not be the best long-term investment for securing your financial independence, but it is a great thing to pass on to your family when the time comes, and it deserves attention when planning the distribution of your estate. [See Chapter 8]

INTANGIBLE PROPERTY INVESTMENTS
(EVERYTHING ELSE EXCEPT REAL ESTATE)

Intangible property is property that lacks a concrete, physical substance, but has a symbolic value. A dollar bill, a share of stock, or a bond is nothing but a piece of paper, but the symbolic value of the piece of paper is usually much more. For example, it may cost 20¢ to print a share of stock, but if you sold that share to someone else, you might receive $75. The money we use everyday has intangible value. Unlike a car, which has a practical purpose, you can't use money for anything except as a medium of exchange. The value of the dollar is always fluctuating, especially in times of inflation and deflation. A hundred dollars went a lot further 75 years ago than it does today.

Basically, there are two types of intangible property: Green Money (safe money) and Red Money (money you can lose).

Green Money (SAFE MONEY)

Green money is safe money. It's money you can bank — basically cash and its equivalents. It only goes up. It never goes down unless you spend it. Types of green money include the following:

1. Savings Accounts: Savings accounts are probably the most common ways people keep their money. When you put your money in a savings account you're giving that money to a bank or credit union to loan out to other people, but the money is still your money and you can take it out any time you want. For example, if you put in $100 dollars today, you're guaranteed to be able to withdraw $100 tomorrow. The bank adds interest to your savings for letting them use your money. The interest amount is usually very small, but generally it keeps the value of your money on par with inflation.

Putting your money away in a savings account has several benefits, the first being security. A government agency known as the Federal Deposit Insurance Corporation (FDIC) insures bank accounts up to $100,000, so even if the local bank where you keep your cash goes under, you're still guaranteed by the federal government to get that money back. Another benefit of keeping money in bank accounts is liquidity: it's easy to convert to cash when you need it. There's no waiting period. Just go to the ATM or bank teller and you can get your money immediately.

One disadvantage to keeping your money in a savings account is the low interest rates. Money in banks almost never dramatically increases in value. The interest you make for letting banks loan your money out to others is a lot less than what they get for lending it. That's the way banks make money. If you have long-term goals for financial independence, you're probably going to want to put some of your savings to work for you in other kinds of investments.

2. CDs: CDs (Certificates of Deposit) are similar to bank accounts, except that they're a lot harder to liquidate when you need the cash quickly. Because they require a longer-term commitment, CDs tend to pay higher interest rates. When you invest in a CD you usually agree to leave that money with the bank for a specific period of time without withdrawing it, frequently two or more years. If you decide, in an emergency, that you absolutely need access to the money you deposited, be prepared to pay a stiff early-withdrawal penalty. Another limitation of both CDs and savings accounts is that the interest you earn on your investment is taxable. Between inflation and these taxes, you're really not making much.

3. Fixed Annuities: An annuity is similar to a bank CD. It's a contract with an insurance company that guarantees your principal and a minimum rate of interest. Annuity accounts can be opened with a single deposit or through a series of deposits. There are various types of annuities, but fixed annuities are the most conservative type.

There are many reasons why people invest their money in fixed annuities. One of those reasons is safety. Like bank CDs, fixed annuities pay the same rate of interest over the life of the contract; this interest tends to be higher than those offered by bank CDs. Some fixed annuities offer the added incentive of being inflation-proof, which means that the fixed rate of interest is adjusted to move up as inflation rates rise. Fixed annuities are also tax-deferred investments, which means taxes are only paid when money is withdrawn from the account. If you are under the age of 59½ there is an IRS early-withdrawal penalty of 10%.

Another feature of fixed annuities is the ability to receive payments at regular intervals, called annuitizing the contract. This can be done in several different ways. An annuity known as a straight life annuity pays a monthly sum until you die. Whatever principal is left over when you die belongs to the life insurance company and cannot be claimed by surviving family members. A refund annuity is an annuity that guarantees that any unpaid portion of the principal remaining in your account at the time of your death gets paid to your heirs. For this feature, you have to pay a bit extra. Another, more costly, type of annuity is the life annuity with term certain. Payments on this annuity are guaranteed for a fixed number of years. If you die before the term expires, the monthly payments continue for your heirs until the time runs out.

Whether or not you choose to annuitize your annuity contract depends a lot on your situation. If you do not have friends, relatives, or charities to whom you want to leave money at the time of your death, purchasing a straight life annuity might make the most sense because you don't have a specific plan for the distribution of your money. You just want to get the highest interest rate you can while you're still alive. If you have family to whom you'd like to leave money when you die, a refund annuity might be the best way to receive a high-interest monthly income and protect your principal at the same time.

Most individuals who own a fixed annuity let the interest accumulate year after year. For example, if you have a $100,000 fixed annuity earning 4%, at the end of the year the account value would be $104,000. That $4,000 gain becomes principal and the next year you would earn 4% on $104,000, and so on.

The gain of $4,000 isn't taxable unless you take it out of the fixed annuity, when it would be taxed as ordinary income. You can control your taxable income using fixed annuities by adjusting the amount you withdraw in a given year. By withdrawing less from an annuity, you can reduce the income tax on your social security benefits, since the tax on social security depends on your other income.

The Newest Fixed Annuity — The Fixed Index Annuity

A new type of annuity allows you to benefit from stock market gains without risking your principal to market fluctuations. The gain you earn on these annuities is linked to increases in a major stock index such as the Standard & Poor's 500 (S&P 500), which is why they're called "equity index" annuities or FIAs. Some FIAs also offer a guaranteed minimum return, which can provide protection in a down market. With FIAs, you have the best of both worlds — the potential for high returns in a rising market and a guaranteed minimum interest rate if the market index declines. Unlike stocks or mutual funds, you don't risk any principal to benefit from a rising stock market. You can make money in an up market like the late '90s, or a down market like we saw in 2000-01.

It's important to understand how Fixed Index Annuities work before jumping in. When you invest in this type of annuity, you're not actually investing in stocks. Instead, you're investing in an annuity whose returns are calculated based on growth in a particular index such as the S&P 500. The S&P 500 index is often used with FIAs and is considered a barometer of stock market performance. From 1998 to

2004, an FIA could outperform the S&P 500 because FIAs provide guaranteed minimum returns even in a down market (see chart). So even if the S&P 500 declined, you would still receive your guaranteed minimum interest rate.

As you can see, Fixed Index Annuities offer many benefits, but they can also be quite complex. Insurance companies can use several different methods to compute annual returns and may offer you a choice among several stock market indexes. In addition, some FIAs cap the amount of growth that can be passed through to you and they usually have a complicated formula for death benefits. You also need to factor in fees and expenses. It's important to consult a qualified agent who is knowledgeable in these concepts if you're considering this type of annuity.

Why Do Retirees Love Tax-Deferred Annuities?

• *Principal Protection: Retirees can use the interest on the annuity as an extra source of income without having to spend down the original amount of their investment, making it possible to pass the remainder of the principal on to loved ones.*

• *Social Security Benefits: The earnings from an annuity are not included in the formula to determine adjusted gross income. This means that any earnings that remain in the annuity contract won't result in increased taxes on Social Security benefits.*

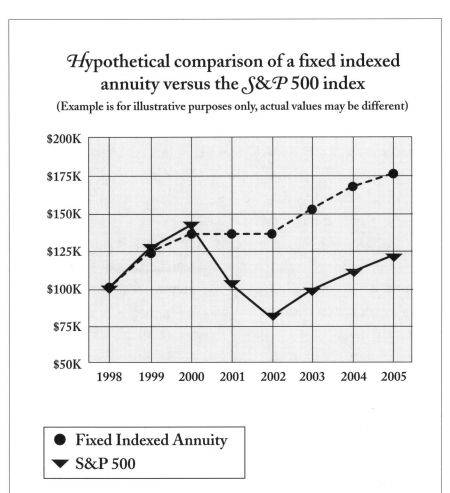

Hypothetical comparison of a fixed indexed annuity versus the S&P 500 index

(Example is for illustrative purposes only, actual values may be different)

- ● **Fixed Indexed Annuity**
- ▼ **S&P 500**

Early withdrawals from annuities may be subject to company withdrawal charges. Withdrawals prior to age 59.5 may also be subject to an IRS tax penalty.

Results are purely hypothetical, and are no indication or guarantee of future performance.

Fixed indexed annuity (FIA) example illustrates an FIA with annual reset and a participation cap of 12%.

"Standard & Poor's," "S&P 500," "Standard & Poor's 500" and "500" are trademarks of The McGraw-Hill Companies, Inc.

Period used for comparison is 9/30/98 through 9/30/05.

Red Money (MONEY YOU CAN LOSE)

Red Money is money you invest. Investing means greater risk, but it also means greater opportunity for return. Red Money investments include the following:

1. Stocks: Stocks are shares of ownership in a company. The values of these shares are tied to the prices on the stock exchange (i.e., NYSE or NASDAQ). Every day, shares of a company's stock are bought and sold for varying prices. The greater the demand there is to own stock from a company, the more valuable one share of ownership in that company becomes. Demand for a stock is usually driven by expectation of future profits. The goal of any investor dealing with stocks is to buy low and sell high. You want someone to pay more for the shares than you did. Because it's difficult to predict movement of stock prices over a short period of time, buying stocks tends to be a medium- to long-range investment. Investing in larger, more established companies is generally less risky and therefore usually results in less variance in stock price over time but also lower overall return.

As investments, stocks have various benefits. The first benefit is the potential for large gain. For example, if you buy 100 shares of a company at $10 a share and those shares go up to $20, you've made a 100% return on your investment. If a company suddenly becomes hot and shares start trading fast, you can sometimes double the value of your investment in a few days or weeks.

Another benefit of investing in stocks is the amount of control you have in deciding what companies to buy into and when to hold or sell. Stocks are generally bought and sold through brokers who act as middlemen in the trading process. Tell a broker to buy or sell 100 shares of any given stock and he or she will go into the market and buy or sell your 100 shares at the market price. In exchange for these services, the broker will charge a commission. Over the years, commission costs have decreased due to discount brokerages and internet trading. These low commission fees have made stocks even more attractive to investors.

Another benefit of stocks is the way they're taxed. The taxes on capital gains (what you make from selling a stock) only have to be paid once you sell your shares, so even if the 100 shares of stock triple in value, that increase does not have to be declared as taxable income until you sell your shares. Capital gains on stocks are taxed at lower rates than other sources of income.

A final benefit of owning stocks is that some stocks pay dividends, which are distributed on a quarterly basis and can be used to supplement your income.

Most disadvantages of investing in stocks have to deal with management of the risk of potential losses. The best scenario for owning stocks is to spread your investments among different sectors and industries so that if one part of the economy struggles, any losses incurred may be offset by gains in other areas. Because you have to pay individual commissions on each trade you make, whether you're buying or selling shares, owning a diverse number of stocks tends to be expensive. Most people can only afford to hold a few individual stocks at a time and thus are subject to more risk if these companies take a plunge.

Stock prices can also be volatile. You can make great returns, but you can also lose a lot as well (note the latest dot-com crash). The risk increases the shorter you hold stocks. For example, if you have $100 invested in a stock that loses 50% of its value and you sell it to pay the bills, you've lost money. If you had held it for another three months and share prices rose again, maybe you would've made money. Overall, investing in stocks requires great vigilance on your part. You not only need to know when to buy and sell but you need to determine how much extra money you can afford to put away in an investment that may take five years to turn a profit. You have to keep your eye on the market and on the economic factors that may influence the price of your shares.

Have Your Cake & Eat It Too

Recently, more and more stock market investors have been putting their money in principal protected investments. These investments, whether in mutual funds or annuity contracts, allow you to invest in equities without the risk of losing principal. Some offer a guaranteed fixed rate of interest. The holding period and fees associated with these investments vary from company to company.

2. **Bonds:** A bond is a written promise to pay on money you lend to someone else. In short, it's an IOU. For example, if you lend money to a government, US or foreign, you get a government bond. If you lend money to a company, like GE or AT&T, you get a corporate bond. If you lend money to a city or municipality, you get a municipal bond.

In selling bonds, borrowers agree to pay back the principal, or the original amount of the loan, by a certain period of time (the maturation date) plus interest, which is paid out in installments to the bondholder. When they are first issued, most bonds have a stated face value — for example, $1,000. This means that when the bond matures, the borrower has to repay the owner the face value of the bond, or $1,000. Most people who own bonds, however, aren't the original holders. Like stocks, bonds are traded in secondary markets at varying prices that depend on the rate of interest that bond will pay the holder. A bond's interest rate is determined by the prevailing federal interest rates at the time the bond is first issued and the credit-worthiness of the borrower. Whatever price you pay for the bond, the borrower only has to pay back the face value of the loan at the time of maturity plus interest.

One of the biggest factors determining the amount of interest paid on a bond is credit risk. Corporate bonds tend to pay higher interest rates because private institutions have a greater risk of bankruptcy or default. A junk bond is a kind of corporate bond issued by a company with a low credit rating and therefore is a bond that pays higher interest rates. Bonds issued by the federal, state, or municipal governments tend to have more conservative rates and less risk, though municipal bonds offer an added incentive because their interest is tax-free. In general, bonds with longer maturity dates pay higher interest rates because they carry more risk of default and require the bondholder to go a longer period of time without being able to cash out.

Bonds have various benefits that make them great investments. Because bonds pay interest on a regular basis, they act as a steady stream of fixed income. Except for junk bonds, which hold a greater chance of default, bonds also tend to be safer investments. On the rare occasion that a bond issuer declares bankruptcy and defaults on the loan, bond holders, as creditors, get first dibs on collecting their money. Stockholders usually wind up with nothing in similar circumstances. Another great feature of a bond is that the principle of the loan gets paid out in full at the time of maturation.

> *Bonds are great for hedging against the volatility of stocks because stocks and bonds tend to run counter to each other in terms of price increases. In a good stock market, bond prices will be low because people will be investing in stocks. Buying bonds cheap will make long-term sense when stock prices drop and bonds again become safe bets for investors.*

Of course bonds have their disadvantages as well. They tend to be interest rate-sensitive. For example, if you're holding a bond that pays an interest rate of 5% and rates go up to 7%, the bond you're holding is going to be harder to sell to anyone else. If rates never drop lower than 5%, you may wind up holding the bond until it matures or selling it at a loss. Bonds, therefore, can't always be sold when you want.

There are several varieties of bonds (corporate, savings, municipal, I-bonds), each with unique benefits and risks. Consult with your financial advisor to determine which type might be an appropriate investment given your circumstances.

> *Bonds can be purchased in various ways — individually, as part of a bond fund, or inside a fixed annuity. Bonds purchased inside a tax-deferred fixed annuity have a principal guarantee feature, which guarantees that the principal invested in the bond can never be lost.*

3. Mutual Funds: Mutual funds are accounts in which investors pool their money together to buy stocks, bonds, or other types of investments. The money is given to a fund manager who decides which assets will make the best investments. The price of a mutual fund is called the Net Asset Value, which is the sum total of all assets in the fund divided by the number of shares in the fund. Different funds focus on different sectors of the economy and therefore carry different degrees of risk. For example, blue chip funds invest only in the big companies that have been around for awhile and will probably have less change in stock price. Growth-funds are generally riskier funds because they focus on companies that hold more potential for profitability than actual return. There are also funds that track the major indexes such as the S&P 500.

As investment vehicles, mutual funds have certain benefits that make them more appealing than just owning individual shares of stocks or bonds. For one thing, mutual funds provide investment diversity. Mutual funds are composites of many shares of different stocks from many different companies. If you were to buy 100 shares of 20 different stocks, the commission costs could be significant, but mutual funds allow you to distribute money across a wide range of companies without these costs. One share of a mutual fund, purchased at the Net Asset Value, may represent a percent ownership in two or three hundred companies. Mutual funds also have the benefit of being managed by a professional who has access to better information about stocks and can keep an eye on your investments for you.

The big downside to mutual funds is the fees. Often there are fees to get in and out of funds (front and back loads) and management fees such as the expense ratio, which pays for professional fund management. Another downside to owning mutual funds is the way they're taxed. Any profit from an investment transaction within the fund sold during the year is taxable as a capital gain even if the overall value of the fund goes down. This means that you sometimes owe a capital gains tax on mutual fund shares that have actually declined in value in the course of the year. For example, if your mutual fund manager sells stocks held by the fund, resulting in a net profit of $10,000, but the fund overall for the year loses $30,000, you will have lost the $30,000 and still owe the capital gains tax on the $10,000.

4. Variable Annuities: Unlike fixed annuities, which pay a fixed rate of interest over time, variable annuities pay interest based on the performance of the principal as it is invested in sub-accounts offered in the annuity contract. Variable annuities can put your money in any number of investments — stocks, bonds, or mutual fund-type accounts in the sub-accounts.

Like fixed annuities, variable annuities are tax-deferred vehicles. Because variable annuity contracts invest your money in riskier types of investments, they offer a potential for greater return than fixed annuities. Like growth earned on fixed annuity accounts, variable annuity earnings can be paid out as income over a fixed period of time or for life, or can be taken out in a lump sum. Some variable annuities offer principal protection features. These accounts are often used by teachers, hospital workers, and state workers as a means to supplement their pensions.

What type of information should I ask before opening an annuity?

- What is the current interest rate?
- Is the principal guaranteed?
- What is the guaranteed rate for the first and subsequent years?
- What are the charges under the contract?
- How many investment choices does the variable annuity offer?
- How will this annuity best serve my needs from an income or estate tax point of view?
- Should I own this annuity individually, jointly, or in a trust? Who should be named as beneficiary? Should I be the recipient of the payments?
- How is the annuity company rated?

REAL ESTATE INVESTMENTS (I CAN'T BELIEVE IT'S WORTH SO MUCH)

The third type of investment property you can own is real estate (i.e., land and buildings). There are basically two types of real estate: residential property and investment property.

Residential Property (BEST INVESTMENT I EVER MADE!)

Residential property is any kind of property you live in and own. In short, it's the place you call home — your slice of the American dream.

There are several reasons why owning your own home is a great idea. One obvious reason is that, as opposed to renting property, which requires that you pay a landlord every month, the money you put into a house or other residence remains your money. Even while you're paying off your mortgage, a percentage of your monthly payments are going toward paying the principal of that loan. When the principal is paid off, you own the property free and clear of the lien created by the mortgage. But even if you don't own the property outright and you're still paying the mortgage, you can sell the property at any time. In that case, whatever percentage of the principal you've paid off plus any appreciation in the value of the real estate becomes your equity in the property. This equity, enhanced by the return of your initial down payment, remains yours to keep (less closing costs for selling the home).

Here's an example: say you buy a house for $300,000 with a down payment of $30,000 and a mortgage of $270,000. At the time of the closing, your equity is only 10% of the value of the house; the bank has a lien against the remainder of the value. If you turn around and sell the house the next day for $310,000, you will only get $40,000 back from the transaction, minus the closing cost, and the bank gets $270,000 to pay off the mortgage. If you sell the house 10 years from now for $400,000 and you've managed to pay off 50% of the mortgage's principal, you get $265,000 from the sale and the bank gets $135,000.

Owning your own home also has certain tax benefits renting does not. Residential properties have tax-deferred growth, which means that like stocks you don't have to pay tax on the increased value of the property until you sell it. Residential properties are also excluded from capital gains tax up to a certain point. Married couples can sell their homes and make up to $500,000 profit without paying a dime in capital gains taxes. For a single person, the tax exemption cut-off is $250,000. In both cases, the owners must have lived in the property for at least two of the last five years. Residential property owners benefit from mortgage interest deduction as well, which means that homeowners can claim income tax deduction on any interest paid on mortgages up to $1 million. Home equity lines of credit up to $100,000 also qualify for this tax deduction.

Another great benefit of owning residential property is the Homestead Exemption, which in Massachusetts protects up to $500,000 of your home equity from attachment by creditors, meaning that creditors will have to go after your other assets. To qualify, a homeowner must file a Homestead Declaration with the appropriate Registry of Deeds.

Condos & Co-ops

A condo is a form of real estate where individual units are owned separately and the property's common areas (parking lot, yard, pool, etc.) are owned jointly by all of the unit owners. Condos have all the benefits of other residential properties. Unit owners, however, are typically required to pay association and other fees that cover common expenses and liabilities and must abide by association rules.

In a co-op, you buy shares of stock in a corporation that owns a building that is subdivided into individual units. Some states consider co-ops real estate; other states treat them like intangible property.

Investment Property
(THE TWO-FAMILY HOME YOU MIGHT HAVE GROWN UP IN)

Investment property is any type of property you purchase or own for the purpose of renting out or selling for profit. Basically, it's real estate that you own as an investment, or to provide income, that's not your residence.

Investment property has several benefits. One benefit is that, like residential property, investment property has tax-deferred growth, which means that you don't have to pay any taxes on appreciation until you sell the place. Another benefit is that by renting out the property instead of living in it, you're able to collect monthly income from the investment.

Investment property has several disadvantages. Like stocks and bonds, investing in property lacks the kind of diversity that allows you to spread out your risk. When you buy a home or a tract of land, you're essentially tying up your money in one asset that can undergo dramatic fluctuation in value based on certain variables. Property is highly interest rate-sensitive. When interest rates are low, more people are buying and financing homes, meaning that demand and price are high. Conversely, when interest rates go up and the cost of loans becomes more expensive, prices of property as a general rule will come down. Also, property is not very liquid — it can't be easily converted to cash.

Another disadvantage of owning investment property is landlord woes. Property doesn't take care of itself, and unless you're handy enough to manage the maintenance work on your own, you'll have to be able to absorb the cost of a management company. You will also bear the cost of major repairs or improvements such as burst pipes, leaky roofs, and elevator installations. Furthermore, as the landlord, people expect you to be on call 24/7. When the toilet won't flush or the water comes out brown, you'll get the call, whether it's two o'clock in the afternoon or two o'clock in the morning.

REITs (pronounced "reets") are another type of real estate investment in property you don't reside in. REITS are essentially the real estate version of a mutual fund. They're "real estate investments trusts" where individual investors pool their money together to buy a portfolio of various properties. These pooled accounts are managed professionally, which of course has associated costs.

Chapter 3

Who Owns My House?
Different Types of Property Ownership

RICH AND SAM ASK:

Do you really care who owns your house? While you're young and mobile you should own it, but when you're older, you don't need to own it — you just need the right to use it.

Both of Sam's parents (his mother is 82 and his father is 91) and Rich's mom (age 89) don't care who owns their homes. All they care about is that 1) they can live there; 2) their home is protected from attachment if they're confined to a nursing home; and 3) when they pass away their home stays in the bloodline. Making sure it's protected and goes to their children and grandchildren is of primary importance.

So all the technical types of ownership might be great to learn about, but the real questions are: what's the bottom line and what do you want to do with the real estate?

Whenever you become a property owner, you're given a title to the property. The title determines who actually owns the property (whether it's you alone or you and your spouse together) and how you're allowed to dispose or transfer the property when you die. The title to real estate is typically shown on the deed, and the title to intangible property can be found on bank records, stock certificates, or some other title transfer document. Basically, there are three ways to title property.

FORMS OF REAL ESTATE TITLES

1. Sole Ownership
In a sole ownership, the title of the property is put in one person's name. One person alone owns the property, and by right can sell it or give it away to whomever they wish without needing anyone else's approval.

2. Joint Ownership
In joint ownership situations, property is owned by two or more people, such as a husband and wife or mother and daughter. There are several different ways of establishing joint ownership rights to an item of property.

Joint Tenants with Right of Survivorship
Under this type of ownership, the property is held in both owners' names. Upon the death of one owner, the surviving owner automatically becomes the sole owner with full rights to sell and give away as he or she pleases. Transfer of the property at death is automatic and avoids probate. This kind of ownership is most commonly

used for a couple's home, but can also be used to title other assets including bank accounts, cars, or personal property assets.

Tenants in Common

Under this kind of ownership, each person owns their own separate share of the whole, which they can sell or transfer without the consent of the other owner(s). The joint owner's interest doesn't automatically pass to a surviving owner at death. This means that each owner has the right to specify how to distribute the property when he or she dies. For example, if you and your brother own investment property and you die, you can transfer your half-ownership directly to your son in your will instead of leaving it to your brother. Because the transfer of property is not automatic, as in the case of Joint Tenants with Right of Survivorship, the property will have to pass through probate.

Community Property

Under this kind of title, all property or earnings acquired by spouses during marriage are considered common property of the marriage, which means that each spouse is entitled to one-half of the property in instances of death or divorce. Here's an example: if you enter into marriage with $100,000 in assets and two years down the road get divorced, your spouse is not usually entitled to the original $100,000. However, if during the two years of marriage you earned $100,000 and purchased a house or invested in other assets, then upon divorce, your spouse is entitled to one-half of that new property acquired during marriage. The only properties exempted from a community property title are gifts and inheritances.

> *Community property derives from Spanish law rather than English Common law and is a type of ownership used in only nine states (Arizona, California, Idaho, Louisiana, Nevada, New Mexico, Texas, Washington, and Wisconsin).*

3. Entity Ownership

You can also title property in the name of a trust or business entity, such as a partnership, corporation, or LLC, that you create with properly-filed formation documents that establish the legality of the entity. Trusts offer many planning opportunities to keep property in your bloodline. [See Chapter 9]

Special Ownership Situations

Prenuptial Agreements

A prenuptial agreement is a legally biding agreement made prior to marriage that determines property ownership rights during and after marriage. Prenuptial agreements are generally used to protect assets or property acquired before marriage from divorce or death. For example, say a wealthy oil tycoon decides to marry his young secretary. In many states, if the couple divorces two years later, the young secretary could claim half of the tycoon's property. If the tycoon is smart, he'll protect his assets prior to the marriage by having his fiancée sign a prenuptial agreement, waving her ownership rights to most of his property.

Prenuptial agreements can supersede community property or joint tenancy, but they have to be enforced by the court, which means that a judge gets the final say on whether or not the prenuptial agreement is deemed fair. In enforcing prenuptial agreements, courts like to see that both sides were represented fairly by an attorney and that both sides gave full disclosure of their assets before signing. But even this doesn't guarantee that the prenuptial agreement will be enforced. In the example of the wealthy tycoon and his young secretary, the young secretary could make the argument that by staying at home during the marriage, or raising children if they had any, she lost out on income she would have made if she were working full time. In this case, a judge may sympathize with the secretary, over-rule the prenuptial agreement, and force the tycoon to pay something to his ex-wife, though the amount would probably not equal half his estate.

Inheritance & Gifts

Property acquired through inheritance or gift is generally considered the sole property of whoever receives it. This doesn't mean that inheritances or gifts are protected from divorce or death. If you leave an inheritance to your child and he or she gets divorced or passes away, that inheritance can pass into the hands of your child's spouse. The best way to insure that the property you leave your children remains in the bloodline is to create a trust that will designate the legal beneficiaries of your inheritance in case of death. [See Chapter 9]

Chapter 4

Insuring Your Family & Your Property Against Unforeseen Circumstances

RICH AND SAM COMMENT:

"I hate insurance companies." How often have we heard that?

Nobody likes to see a cold corporation controlling their monetary future with arbitrary regulations, but unfortunately the only way to protect against disaster is to insure against loss. Most houses don't burn down, but you still wouldn't go without fire insurance for your home, right? Insurance companies are a part of life whether we like it or not. In making sure your assets stay in the bloodline and are protected, you may have to use their services.

Life insurance has been used for decades as a means of transferring tax-free wealth.

Remember not to overbuy, and make sure that if you cancel you get all your money back. Not all insurance works this way but it's getting there. And keep in mind that you can insure your money the same way you can insure your home.

We all want to protect the things we own and minimize the risk of losing the things that are vital to our well-being. The world is an unpredictable place, and as someone with income and investments, you want to have insurance that will protect these assets from being completely wiped out if a tragedy were to occur.

LIFE INSURANCE

Life insurance provides money for your family if you die, to replace the money you would have earned if you were still living and working. It can also cover the cost of burial and help pay the taxes and administrative fees required to settle your estate. Life insurance pays a lump sum amount at the time of your death, and although this money isn't subject to income tax, it is subject to estate tax. With the proper planning, though, these taxes can be reduced, leaving your family in a more comfortable and secure position.

In determining how much life insurance you need, it's important to ask yourself the following questions:

- **How much income am I trying to replace?** Obviously, when you die, your employment income will stop. In determining how much life insurance to purchase, you need to calculate the amount of income your family would need if you died suddenly. You also have to consider how much money your family would need to preserve your current standard of living. If you buy a $1 million policy for your family, when you die that $1 million will probably be invested in something to create a steady stream of yearly income to support your family. The amount of insurance coverage you purchase will depend partly on how much return you anticipate your family can get when they invest it after your death. You want the money you leave them to grow over time. The more coverage you provide, the more income they can earn from their investments, and this will keep them from having to dip into their reserve or spend down the principal.

- **What type of special expenses do I need to be concerned about?** Depending on your life situation at the time of your death, you may need to purchase a life insurance policy that covers extra expenses like your children's educations or weddings. For this reason, you may want to purchase additional amounts of coverage that provide extra for emergencies.

- **Do you own a business?** If you own a small business and you die, your family or business partner is going to need cash to cover liabilities for that business. If you have a business partner, a life insurance policy can enable your partner to purchase your share of the business from your family, giving your relatives an additional nest egg.

Types of Life Insurance

There are four types of life insurance policies: term life, whole life, variable life, and universal life.

1. Term Life: Term life insurance policies pay a death benefit if you die during a specified period of time, typically one year. The policy's premium, or what it costs to buy and renew the policy, is determined by your health, age, and the benefit amount of the policy being purchased. The amount of the premium usually increases as you age. Some policies, however, offer level premiums that are guaranteed not to go up for a certain number of years. With these policies, you pay more when you're younger but save money on premiums when you're older.

The disadvantage of buying some term life policies is that when the term expires, you don't get any money back if you've survived the term of the policy. This kind of term insurance policy therefore has no cash value. These policies don't represent any actual money while you hold them. They can't be converted to cash and your family only gets the money when you die so you can't borrow against them to make other purchases. Some employers offer term life insurance through group policies, which generally makes them less expensive to purchase.

> *You can purchase term life insurance policies where the premium is guaranteed for 5, 10, 15, 20, or 30 years. You can also find some policies that offer a return-of-premium feature. This means that if you pay $1,000 a year into a 30-year policy, you'll receive $30,000 back after 30 years if the policy has gone unused.*

2. Whole Life: Whole life, or ordinary life, insurance offers two things: an insurance policy that pays out upon your death, and an investment component that allows part of the premium you pay to grow tax-free until it's withdrawn. Whole life policies have higher premiums that remain constant, but they also pay dividends much like stocks do. Over time, if the investment component of the policy yields enough return, the dividends can cancel out the premium payments to the point that you're getting life coverage without paying any premium at all. The cash value grows at a specified (fixed) rate, which is guaranteed by the insurance provider.

Another great benefit of whole life policies is that they have a cash value you can borrow against just as you might borrow against the equity in your home. Because you're paying a premium over and above what you would pay for term life, this extra premium gets put into an account that has real cash value. In some cases, you can transfer that money into an annuity to generate income. When you die, your family has the benefit of both the proceeds from the policy and the investment component, which will provide them with more financial security.

3. Variable Life: Variable life insurance is similar to whole life insurance, except that it allows the policy-holder to invest the accumulated cash value in mutual fund-type investments instead of a guaranteed fixed return. Variable life offers the potential for greater returns on investment, while exposing the policy-holder to greater market risk.

4. Universal Life: Universal life insurance is similar to variable life except that the investment component is in bonds (or similar low risk investments), rather than mutual fund-type investments. Universal life therefore offers the option of combining term insurance with permanent (whole life) insurance, thereby reducing premiums and still having a guaranteed death benefit. Universal life typically has a larger savings component than whole life, and also gives the policy holder the benefit of flexible premiums. However, lower premiums reduce the cash value of the policy.

What's a Guarantee of Death Benefit?

A guarantee of death benefit means that the death benefit, or amount paid to survivors upon the death of the insurance policy holder, is permanently fixed and therefore cannot be affected by the policy's investment performance. Guarantees of death benefit are most commonly offered by whole life and universal life policies.

OTHER KINDS OF INSURANCE

In addition to life insurance, which protects your family at the time of your death, there are types of insurance that cover disability, property damage, legal liabilities, medical care, and nursing home costs.

Disability Insurance

Disability insurance replaces income lost when you can't work due to illness or injury. This kind of insurance may be provided by an employer but shouldn't be confused with worker's compensation insurance, which only covers injuries that happen within the scope of your employment. The amount of benefit paid on disability insurance varies, but it can be as high as two-thirds of your income. The premium, or cost for this insurance, also varies depending on the benefit amount you want the insurance to pay. There can also be a waiting period of 90-180 days before you can start collecting.

Long-Term Care Insurance

Long-term care insurance covers long-term medical care in situations when health problems are extreme and you're forced to go into a nursing home or assisted living facility. Long-term care insurance is purchased to provide benefits for things that Medicare doesn't cover. Medicare benefits don't begin until age 65 and help pay for hospitals and doctors, but only cover nursing home care for 100 days. Having supplemental long-term care insurance is important because it allows you to protect yourself and your spouse against the costs of nursing home care, which can reach rates of $150-$250 or more per day depending on the location and the facility.

The benefits paid out on a long-term care insurance policy depend on the coverage you've purchased. Some policies have inflation protection built in, which adjusts the amount of the benefit according to increases in nursing home prices and cost of living.

Getting long-term care insurance is a particularly good idea if you don't want to go on Medicaid, which requires that you spend down all your assets until you qualify for assistance.

There's a new generation of long-term care insurance policies that provide a return-of-premium feature if you don't use the policy.

Property Insurance

Property insurance, or homeowner's insurance, covers property loss and injuries that occur on the premises. Depending on the type of policy you buy, and the premium you pay, damages can be covered in one of two ways. If you pay a higher premium, you can get a replacement cost policy that covers the cost to repair the damages and return your property to its original condition. The other option is to purchase a cash value policy that only covers the value of the damaged property. Although the premiums are generally lower on this kind of policy, the benefits may not cover the real expenses of repairing the damages, especially if construction prices go up.

> *There are also property insurance policies that cover special items like jewelry, antiques, furniture, and art, in case they're stolen or damaged.*

Umbrella Insurance Policies (EVERYBODY SHOULD HAVE ONE)

Umbrella insurance policies are insurance policies that cover liability judgments or legal fees that are above the limits of your other insurance policies.

For example, if you're having a party and a guest trips on the rug and breaks his collar bone, that guest might turn around and sue you for damages. Depending on the judgment of the court, you may wind up paying hospital bills and legal fees. Some property and homeowner insurance policies will cover you for these liabilities, but if the bills and fees exceed the amount covered by your policy, you'll have to pay the difference on your own. By purchasing an additional umbrella policy, you give yourself a little added protection against the unforeseen for a relatively low premium.

Chapter 5

Retirement Planning
(So What Am I Going to Do and
Will I Have Enough to Do It?)

Rich Remarks:

It might sound simple, but the most important aspect of retirement planning is making sure you don't lose the principal. Our parents really got it right: it doesn't matter that they earn 3% on a bank CD... what matters is that they didn't lose 20% in a mutual fund.

Why, when we see or hear from a "wise man," is the wise man always old? Well, it's simple. Older individuals have seen it all. So when our parents give advice — take it! They've seen it all!

Retirement planning is a crucial part of determining what your state of financial independence will be down the road. You may have enough to live on now, but what's going to happen when you stop working, or your other assets dry up? You need to have a plan for the future.

Determining what your plan will be requires three considerations:

- **Determine how much income you'll need to cover your living expenses when you retire:** How much will you need to support your lifestyle after retirement? What will your fixed expenses be? How much do you want to stash away for vacations, luxury items, and rainy days? How much do you want to leave behind for your children and grandchildren?

- **Decide how much you need to be saving now in order to reach your goal:** If you're still working, what's the right amount of money to save for future expenses in retirement?

- **Do not count on social security as a fall-back plan:** Once a safety net for so many elderly and retired persons, economic and demographic factors have made the future of social security uncertain. Be aware that benefits may be reduced in the long-term as the number of recipients increases compared to the number of workers contributing. [See Social Security Reform sidebar in Chapter 1]

If you're nearing or beginning retirement now, the future is already upon you. Maybe you've discovered that those Social Security checks just aren't going to cut it. At this point, you should probably consider finding an investment, like an annuity, that can give you the benefits of principle protection while offering a rate of interest that can be used for supplemental monthly income.

THE RETURN-ON-PRINCIPAL FORMULA

Most retirees don't want to spend down, or exhaust, their life savings during their retirement. They want to use their life savings as principal on which they can earn interest that acts as a second or third source of income for them. How much extra income will you need to support yourself without having to dip into your life savings? Well, that depends on two things:

- **How much you'll spend:** This can be difficult to determine. The older you get, the more expensive things get. Plus you need to consider the rising costs of health care and nursing homes.

- **How much you'll have coming in:** Unless you plan to work part-time during your retirement, most of your income will probably be generated from sources like pensions and Social Security (knock on wood!!).

The difference between what you need to support your lifestyle and what you'll have as income will give you a general idea of the nature of the investment you'll need to make to protect whatever savings you already have.

For example, let's say you retire at the age of 65 with $600,000 in the bank. If you spend $50,000 a year and have a net income of $20,000, you'll need to find investments that provide you with a combined return on principal of at least 5% a year, or $30,000, without being forced to spend down. If you've only saved $300,000 by the time of retirement, you'll need a return of 10%.

Of course, this formula doesn't factor in inflation or emergency costs, but it can give you a rough idea of how much you need to save and what kind of returns you'll need on any future investments you make.

Always count on needing more money when you retire because you'll have more free time in which to spend your money.

The Income for Life Model™

In 1984, Philip G. Lubinski, CFP, a financial advisor from Denver, CO, developed a retirement distribution model he called Income for Life.

We have worked with Phil for some time to perfect the Income for Life Model™. The Model seeks to provide continuing, inflation-adjusted income to last throughout retirement. We realize that unless retirees invest their assets in a manner that focuses on delivering reliable streams of income, they run the risk of losing their investment principle.

We have discovered that the secret of investing success for older Americans is not found in timing *the market, but rather is a function of* time in *the market. The strategy of Income for Life is to provide inflation-adjusted income for life.*

The Income for Life Model™ is a strategic combination of asset allocation and product selection. A retiree deposits designated funds that are allocated to six "buckets" that will hold invested assets ranging from very conservative to aggressive. Each bucket is turned into an income stream for a five-year period. Having six buckets in different asset allocations provides for inflation-adjusted monthly income for at least 30 years.

TYPES OF RETIREMENT PLANS

There are basically two types of retirement plans you can use to save money: employer-provided plans and individual plans.

Employer-Provided Plans

Employer-provided plans are retirement plans offered as a benefit by the company you work for. These plans vary from employer to employer, but there are basically two types.

1. Defined Benefit Plans & Pension Plans: These plans are becoming rare in private industry, but are still widely used for public employees, such as state workers, teachers, police, and firemen. With these plans, your employer usually pays a specific benefit, or amount, at a monthly rate for the rest of your life. The benefit is determined by the number of years you worked for your employer and your salary. Some defined benefit plans have cost of living adjustments, or COLAS, built into them, which will increase the benefit they pay you based on the inflation rate so that the benefit keeps up with rising prices and the general cost of living.

The amount of benefit you receive is also influenced by what happens to your plan when you die. For instance, most plans will continue to pay 100, 75, or 50% of your benefits to your spouse after you die for the rest of his/her life. These options must be carefully chosen prior to retirement. These plans usually allow your spouse to wave the survivor benefit, which in turn results in a higher benefit payment while both you and your spouse are still alive. Of course, by waving this right for the higher benefit, your spouse receives nothing when you die.

2. Defined Contribution Plan: These are plans that you contribute to while you're still working for your employer and are more commonly known as 401(k)s, or 403(b)s for non-profit employers. With the defined contribution plan, the benefit you receive in retirement is determined by how much you set aside in your own account every paycheck. In essence, you pay now to have security for the future.

The advantage of defined contribution retirement plans, or 401(k)s, is that the money you contribute to your account is often invested by your employer in mutual funds or stocks and grows tax-deferred until you start to withdraw it. In some plans, a percentage of the contribution you make to your own account is matched by your employer's own contribution. This depends on how your employer's plan is structured. With defined contribution plans, you're required to begin withdrawing a minimum amount (minimum distribution requirement) from your account by the age of 70½. You do have options for withdrawal: you can either draw the money out in a lump sum (which might put you in a higher income tax bracket); you can have the amount distributed over your life-expectancy and thus spread out the tax payments at a lower tax rate; or you can choose somewhere in between, depending on your income needs.

There are usually other features that govern defined contribution plans. For example, though you're always guaranteed to be able to withdraw your own contribution from the account, you may not be able to withdraw your employer's contributions until you've worked at that company for a minimum number of years (known as vesting). If you leave a company before you retire, you're usually able to bring your 401(k) with you to your new job, roll it into your IRA (see below), or simply withdraw it. By withdrawing it, you'll have to pay taxes. When transferring your 401(k) to your new employer's plan or to your IRA, make sure that your money gets transferred directly to a retirement account to avoid negative tax consequences. Some companies allow an "in-service" distribution where you can roll-over (tax-free) a portion of your 401(k) to a self-directed IRA.

It is a good idea to make sure that you diversify your 401(k) investments. Some employers put all their employees' 401(k) options into company stock, which can lead to financial ruin if the industry takes a down-turn or a problem develops within the company, such as what happened to the employees of Enron.

Individual Plans

Individual retirement plans are plans that are not offered through an employer. These are plans you create yourself, either because you're self-employed or because your employer doesn't offer a retirement plan as a benefit. There are three types of individual retirement plans:

1. Traditional IRAs (Individual Retirement Account): With a traditional IRA, you're allowed to contribute up to $4,000 annually to your account without paying taxes on it. Whether or not you qualify for this tax deduction depends on your annual income and whether or not your employer offers a retirement plan.

The big advantage of IRAs is that the money you put in the account grows tax-deferred until withdrawal. Like 401(k)s, you must begin withdrawing a minimum amount from the account when you turn 70½. You are also allowed to choose a lump sum payment, payments spread out over the rest of your life, or somewhere in between. If you choose to withdraw the money in a lump sum, you have to pay the taxes all at once. If you choose to receive the payments spread out over the rest of your life, you'll pay taxes for each installment on an annual basis. Whatever is withdrawn from the IRA is taxable as ordinary income.

2. Roth IRA: Another type of IRA is the Roth IRA. The Roth IRA has the same annual contribution amounts as normal IRAs, but without the up front tax deductions. With a Roth IRA you pay your taxes up front, instead of waiting until you begin withdrawing funds, as is the case for the traditional IRA. The amount in the account grows tax-free and by paying the taxes up front, you don't have to pay taxes when you withdraw, which may wind up saving you money depending on your tax brackets.

3. Annuities: Individual retirement plans can also involve annuities. Annuities are great for retirement because you're not limited in the amount you can put away tax-deferred. Based on the type of annuity you choose, you can put your money in any number of investments — stocks, bonds, or mutual funds. Annuities also give you the option of turning the interest you've earned on investments into income you can spread out over the rest of your life.

Part II

Estate Planning:
How to Protect Your
Wealth & Pass It On

Chapter 6

Taxes: The Government Gets its Piece

RICH REFLECTS:

We all know the old adage — you can't escape death and taxes.

Well, we can't escape death, but we sure can escape taxes! If there's anything that bugs my mom a lot more than insurance, it's taxes. Growing up during the Depression when salaries were $35 a week, she finds it hard to be paying more than that amount for just their real estate tax, a payment that can't be avoided.

*But taxes on earned interest, and certainly death taxes, **can** be avoided. Just ask my mom.*

I n America, we pay taxes on the wealth we earn, whether it's income from a job, rent from a tenant, or interest from a bank account. We also pay taxes on the wealth we pass along to others — in the form of gift or inheritance taxes.

It's important to take these transfer taxes into consideration when you're planning to leave a house or stocks to your loved ones, or when you're thinking of giving children or grandchildren money for their education.

THE GIFT AND ESTATE TAX CREDITS

Under the current transfer tax system, you're allowed to give away certain amounts of assets during your life and at death tax-free. The Gift Tax Credit is a term that refers to the amount of money or other property you're allowed to give away to others during your lifetime without owing a tax on the transfer. The Estate Tax Credit refers to the value of assets you can pass on to family and friends after your death without paying any estate taxes.

Through the Gift Tax Credit, the federal government allows you to give a total of $1 million worth of tax-free gifts during your lifetime. This means that the government is empowered to tax you on any gift you make that brings you above that $1 million lifetime maximum, unless the gift is made tax-free by some other special exemption (see below).

The Estate Tax Credit applies to your estate after you die; currently it allows you to pass on up to $2 million in wealth without paying any estate taxes on the transfer. Any amount of your estate that is transferred after your death over the $2 million maximum will be subject to taxation.

> **Example:** When Al gave $200,000 in GM shares and his vacation home, valued at $280,000, to his children three years ago, that $480,000 transferred tax-free because the transfer amount was under the $1 million Gift Tax Credit cap. If Al dies in 2006, his estate will be allowed to pass to his children without incurring an estate tax liability as long as the value of his estate (assets he owned at the time of his death) is less than the Estate Tax Credit of $2 million.

Phase Out

While it has been said that death and taxes are the only sure things in life, it's never certain how much you'll wind up paying in taxes when you die. That's because the government frequently changes the tax laws and the amount you're allowed to exclude, or protect, from taxes. In the next couple of years, the estate and gift taxes will undergo some dramatic changes. In 2009, the federal government is going to increase the Estate Tax Credit to $3.5 million. The Gift Tax Credit will remain at $1 million. In 2010, the estate tax is going to phase out all together, only to re-emerge again in 2011 at the $1 million level. What happens after that is a mystery, which makes planning now for your estate that much more uncertain.

The Credit for Estate and Gift Taxes is Increased

The Gift Tax Credit exempts the first $1,000,000 of transfers made during life. For 2006, the Estate Tax Credit exempts the first $2,000,000 of wealth transfers made at death. This amount will increase as follows:

Year	Estate Tax Exemption	Maximum Tax Rates
2006	$2 million	46%
2007	$2 million	45%
2008	$2 million	45%
2009	$3.5 million	45%
2010	n/a (taxes repealed)	35% (gift tax only)
2011 & beyond	$1 million	55%

The Gift Tax

A gift tax is a tax you pay when you transfer assets (property, money, stocks, bonds, jewelry, etc.) to someone else during your lifetime. The gift must be accepted for it to count as a valid transaction. Once the gift is given, the gift-giver assumes primary responsibility for any taxes that need to be paid.

Under the current law, you're allowed to pass a total of $1 million worth of assets to someone else tax-free. This level has been fixed by Congress and is expected to remain the same for many years to come.

There are several special gift tax exemptions that do not count against the $1 million lifetime cap:

1. **Annual exemptions:** You're allowed to gift $12,000 per recipient every year without paying a gift tax (married couples are allowed to gift $24,000 per recipient). If you make gifts above that amount, you must file a gift tax return (known as a Form 709). Only gifts above $12,000 will count against your $1 million lifetime gift tax exemption.

> **Example:** If Fred has two children, three grandchildren, and one nephew, he could give each of them $12,000 in one year without filing forms or paying taxes on the total gifted amount of $72,000. If Fred decides the next year to give his vacation home, valued at $300,000, to his two children, Fred would have to file a gift tax form because the value of the gift for gift tax purposes would be $276,000 ($300,000 — (2 x $12,000)). The $276,000 would reduce his $1 million lifetime exclusion to $724,000.

2. Education exemptions: You're allowed to gift an unlimited amount of money to someone without paying a gift tax as long as that money is paid directly to an educational institution for the cost of tuition. This exemption applies to tuition alone and can't be used to pay for room and board, meal plans, or books.

> **Example:** Barbara would like to pay for her granddaughter Emma's college education. The tuition for Emma's school costs $25,000 per year. Barbara has two options: she could give Emma $25,000 at the beginning of every school year to put towards her tuition, or Barbara could pay $25,000 directly to the school on behalf of Emma. If Barbara chooses the first option, she will have to file a gift tax return and $13,000 ($25,000-$12,000) will count towards her lifetime gift tax exemption; if she chooses the latter option and pays the $25,000 directly to the school, the entire amount is tax-free.

3. Medical care exemptions: You're allowed to gift an unlimited amount of money to someone without paying a gift tax as long as that money is paid directly to a health care provider (hospital or doctor) for the purpose of covering medical expenses (diagnosis, treatment, and cure of disease). The exemption does not include amounts reimbursed by health insurance benefits.

> **Example:** Frank's nephew severely breaks his leg and is hospitalized for three days. Frank's nephew has no health insurance and his final bill amounts to $15,000. If Frank pays the hospital bill directly, on behalf of his nephew, the entire transaction passes tax-free. If Frank decides instead to give his nephew the money to pay for the bill, Frank must file a

form 709, and $3,000 ($15,000-$12,000) will count against his lifetime gift tax exemption.

4. Spousal exemptions: You're allowed to gift an unlimited amount to your spouse without paying a gift tax as long as your spouse is a US citizen and you're legally married at the time of the gift. If your spouse is not a US citizen, you're only allowed to transfer $100,000 per year without it counting towards your lifetime gift tax exemption.

5. Life insurance exemptions: You're allowed to transfer a life insurance policy to someone without paying gift or estate taxes as long as the cash value of the policy (whatever's been earned from its investment component) is under $12,000 and the policy is transferred at least three years before you die. If you die within three years of transferring your policy to someone else, the policy's benefit is includable in your estate for estate tax purposes.

> **Example:** Joe decides to transfer his $1 million life insurance policy to his nephew Mike. Because the policy only has $5,000 in cash value, Joe doesn't have to pay a gift tax on the transfer. If Joe dies one year later, the $1 million benefit Mike receives is taxable as part of Joe's total estate. But if Joe dies three years and one month after transferring the policy, the entire $1 million passes gift and estate tax free.

6. Minor children exemptions: You may not want to gift large amounts of money to minor children outright because they won't know what to do with it and might not make good management decisions. Instead, you can set up something known as a custodial account at a bank, which allows you to gift up to $12,000 per year tax-free until the child reaches the age of 18. Once the child reaches 18, he or she can access the account without incurring a gift tax. You can also create something called a minor's trust, or 2503(c) trust, which distributes principal and interest to the beneficiaries when they turn 21. You're allowed to put up to $12,000 in this trust each year without filing a gift tax return.

Gift/Tax Liability

Gift	Tax Liability
You give your grandchild a $7,000 ring for Christmas.	None. The value of the ring is under $12,000.
You and your spouse give your daughter $100,000 towards a down payment on a house.	$76,000. You're allowed to gift $24,000 per recipient as a couple each year. $100,000-$24,000=$76,000, which is counted against your $1 million dollar lifetime gift tax exclusion.
You give Harvard $25,000 to pay for your grandson's first year of tuition.	None. As long as you send the $25,000 check directly to Harvard, you're not subject to a gift tax.
You give your nephew a $35,000 car.	$23,000 subject to gift tax ($35,000-$12,000, the annual exemption).
You give your spouse a $35,000 car.	None. Married couples can gift an unlimited amount to each other.
You have $220,000 you want to spread out to your 22 grandchildren. You give each grandchild $10,000.	None. You can gift an unlimited amount of money per year as long as individual amounts do not exceed $12,000 per recipient.

THE FEDERAL ESTATE TAX

The federal estate tax is a tax based on the value of total property you transfer at the time of your death. Unlike an inheritance tax, which draws directly from the beneficiary, or person inheriting property or money, the estate tax is paid from the value of the estate itself, before the assets and property are transferred to the beneficiaries. Even if your property avoids probate and passes directly to your beneficiaries through a trust or will, it's still subject to the federal estate tax.

Determining Your Gross Estate

To find out how much you're going to pay in estate taxes, you need to first determine the value of your gross estate (i.e., the total fair market value of all your assets and property at the time of death).

The following types of property are included in your gross estate and are therefore subject to the estate tax upon certain conditions:

• All property owned exclusively by you at the time of your death, including tangible (furniture, antiques, jewelry), intangible (stocks, bonds, mutual funds), and real estate.

• Insurance, if owned at death or transferred within three years prior to your death.

• Annuities, unless they're straight life annuities, which terminate upon death.

- Property where you have a retained life estate (i.e., property that you've transferred to another person but have retained a right to possession during your lifetime).

- Property owned with your spouse. If you own community property, 50% of that property is taxable as part of your estate. However, when the property is owned by tenants in common (father/son, boyfriend/girlfriend, etc.) the entire property is subject to estate tax, unless the surviving tenant in common can provide evidence that he or she made contributions to the purchase of the property.

> *Remember, all assets are subject to the estate tax, even if they avoid probate.*

Estate Tax Deductions

There are certain deductions that allow you to limit the amount of estate tax liability by reducing your gross estate.

- Marital deduction: The marital deduction allows you to pass an unlimited amount of property to your surviving spouse tax-free.

- Charitable deduction: The charitable deduction allows you to transfer assets to a charity without being subject to an estate tax. Most colleges, libraries, and hospitals qualify as charitable organizations. Consult the I.R.S. for the full list of recognized charities.

• Estate expense and liability deductions: Estate expenses (cost of funeral, lawyers, probate) or liabilities such as debts are also treated as deductions that can be subtracted from the total amount of your gross estate.

Estate Tax Rates

Estate tax rates are determined by the total value of your estate. Generally, they tend to be higher than individual tax rates. Like estate tax exemptions, estate tax rates change frequently. Currently, federal estate tax rates range from 41-46% (46% being the maximum rate applied to any estate). In 2009, the maximum tax rate will decrease to 45%. In 2010, the rate will drop to 0% when the estate tax disappears, before jumping up to 50% beginning in 2011.

Sample calculation: To see the estate tax in action, let's look at a sample calculation based on 2006 tax rates.

A single man named Al owns the following property at the time of his death:

House	$800,000
Bank account	$100,000
Stocks	$300,000
Bonds	$400,000
Life insurance	$1 million

Total Gross Estate	$2.6 million

Because there are deductions that factor into the estate tax equation, Al's estate doesn't have to pay taxes on this gross amount. If Al donates $100,000 to a charity, owes $75,000 on his mortgage, and his estate winds up paying $25,000 for funeral costs and lawyer fees, this $200,000 would be deducted from Al's gross estate to produce a final taxable amount of $2.4 million.

Based on the prevailing I.R.S. estate tax rates, an estate worth $2.4 million would end up owing $184,000 in taxes after the $2 million Estate Tax Credit is deducted from the total.

STATE DEATH TAX

Like income taxes, estate taxes are also paid out on a state level at various rates depending on the state in which you reside. Some states use something known as the sponge tax (Massachusetts followed this approach until recently). Sponge taxes literally "sponge off" the amount of taxes the federal government takes from your estate. A portion of the federal estate tax (typically around 10%) is treated as a state tax credit, which is subsequently soaked up by the state government. The upside to the sponge tax was that it didn't increase the amount your estate paid in taxes — it just took a little from what was already going to the federal government.

With the passage of the 2001 tax bill, the federal government phased out the state death tax credit in 2005. This means that the state governments will either impose their own estate tax system or abandon the state death tax altogether. This "decoupling" of the state death tax from the federal estate tax will probably result in states determining their own estate tax credit amounts as well.

For 2006, Massachusetts enacted a new estate tax system that has an estate tax credit of $1 million (compared to the federal credit of $2 million). This means that a person dying in 2006 could be exempt from federal estate taxes but still owe a Massachusetts estate tax.

THE GENERATION-SKIPPING TAX

The generation-skipping tax (GST) is a tax on assets over $1 million transferred over two generations (eg., grandparent to grandchild). The tax penalizes attempts to bypass the double-taxation of the estate when it passes from the first generation (parent) to the second (child) and then to the third (grandchildren). Because the generation-skipping tax is added to the estate and gift tax, it can be a costly drain on your estate.

The current law allows you to transfer $1 million in property to the third generation without paying generation-skipping taxes. As the tax exemptions amount changes in the next few years, the generation skipping tax exemption amount will follow, disappearing entirely in 2010 and returning again in 2011.

CAPITAL GAINS TAX

A capital gains tax is a tax on profits earned from the sale of investments. These include sale of stocks, bonds, mutual funds, or houses. They're filed as part of your yearly income tax return.

To compute capital gain, you subtract the cost basis (or cost of buying the asset) from the selling price (amount realized).

Capital gains are triggered by a realization event — typically the sale of the asset. A capital loss occurs when you lose money on the sale of an investment. Capital losses can be treated as deductions on your yearly income tax return.

The cost basis of an asset (used to calculate capital gain or loss) is determined by how you acquire the asset. There are three ways you can acquire an asset:

1. Purchasing the asset: If you purchase the asset, the cost basis is the price of the asset at the time of purchase, including any commissions and associated expenses.

> **Example:** If you purchase 100 shares of stock for $50 a share plus the $9.95 broker's commission, your cost basis would be $5,009.95. If you subsequently sold those shares for $90 a share your capital gain would equal the selling price minus cost basis, which would be $9,000-$5,009.95=$3,990.05.

2. Receiving the asset as a gift: If you receive the asset as a gift, there are three scenarios that decide cost basis:

a) If you're selling the gift at a gain and it was given to you at a gain, you use the carry-over basis, which means you take the donor's cost basis (what they paid for it).

> **Example:** If a father gives a son land that the father originally purchased for $40,000, but is now worth $90,000 at the time

of the gift, the son's cost basis is $40,000. If the son later sells the land for $100,000, he has a $60,000 capital gain.

(b) If you receive the gift at a gain, but are selling it at a loss, the cost basis for the person receiving the gift is the carry-over basis (the donor's basis).

> **Example:** A father gives a son land worth $90,000 at the time of the gift, which he originally purchased for $40,000. The son later sells the land for $25,000. The loss would be $40,000-$25,000, or $15,000.

c) If you receive the gift at a loss and sell it at a loss, you use the fair market value (fmv) of the asset at the time of gift to compute the loss.

> **Example:** A father gives a son land worth $30,000 at the time of the gift, which he originally purchased for $40,000. The son later sells the land for $25,000. Using the fair market value of the land at the time of the gift, the loss would equal $30,000-$25,000, or $5,000.

If you have to use the fair market value at the time of the gift to compute the loss, you'll need to obtain the value of the asset on the date of the gift. In the case of stocks, you need to be aware of stock splits or dividends that may put the stock at a value different from the current listed price. You should research the stock price to determine the correct value.

3. Inheriting the asset: If you inherit the asset, you receive what's known as a "stepped-up basis," which means that your cost basis is the fair market value of the asset at the date of the death of the person who left the asset to you.

> **Example:** Al bought stock in 1970 for $50,000. When Al's son inherits that stock in 2003 upon Al's death, the shares are now valued at $225,000. If a year later Al's son decides to sell that stock for $250,000, under current tax law he only has to pay taxes on a capital gain of $25,000. On the other hand, if Al had gifted that stock to his son while he was still alive and his son sold it in 2004 for $250,000, Al's son would have had to pay taxes on all gains earned between 1970 and 2004, or $200,000.

In certain cases, the executor will choose "an alternate valuation date" — six months from the date of death — for estate tax purposes. The executor must notify the beneficiaries in this case.

Changes in the Stepped-Up Basis

Beginning in 2004, the federal estate tax credit amount increased, and will continue to do so, until the estate tax phases out altogether in 2010. In 2011, unless Congress decides otherwise, the estate tax credit will return to the 2001 level of $1 million.

The way capital gains taxes are determined on inherited assets will also change over the course of the next few years. Under current law, assets transferred to beneficiaries are treated with a stepped-up cost basis, which means that beneficiaries only have to pay taxes on any capital gains earned on an asset from the time they inherited it to the time they sell it.

From now until 2010, there will be no limit to the amount of stepped-up cost basis any beneficiary can receive when inheriting an asset. In 2010, when the estate tax phases out, the stepped-up cost basis will be limited to $3 million for the surviving spouse and $1.3 million for all other beneficiaries.

Capital Gains for Homeowners

There are special capital gains tax rules for homeowners. If you own and have lived in a home for two of the previous five years, you can exclude gains (profits) of up to $250,000 if you're single and $500,000 if you're married and filing a joint tax return.

To calculate the gain on your home, take the home's selling price minus the cost basis and any closing costs (broker's fees, title insurance, lawyer fees, inspection, etc.). The cost basis is your original purchase price plus any capital improvements (e.g., you built an addition on to the house).

If you've lived in your home for less than two years, as a homeowner you may qualify for a reduced exclusion if you sell it. The IRS issued regulations in December 2002 that spell out the following "safe harbors:" selling due to change of employment, health reasons, or "unforeseen circumstances" (such as death, loss of job, divorce, or terrorist attack).

Chapter 7

Probate: What's the Hold Up Anyway?

RICH REFLECTS:

Did Rose Kennedy own anything at her death? Most likely. Will we ever know? Nope. Why? Her estate avoided probate.

Probate is public, expensive, time consuming, and you might have to hire a lawyer to get you through it. So why do so many people set up their estate so it will go through probate? I just don't know.

There are so many inexpensive ways to avoid probate that are so easy to implement you can actually do it yourself.

Probate is a legal proceeding conducted by a state court that oversees and manages the distribution of your property after you die. Probate rules vary from state to state, but the main purpose of probate is to clear title of ownership on your property so that it can pass from you to your beneficiaries as dictated by your will or by the laws of intestacy, if you don't have a will. The probate process ends in a decree from the court that provides evidence that title has transferred and ensures that the property goes to those family members and loved ones you want to receive it.

> *If you don't have a will, your estate will be distributed by the courts according to the laws of intestacy. These laws, which vary from state to state, determine who will receive your property at the time of your death and the amount each living beneficiary is entitled to receive.*

The four main steps to the probate process:

1. The will is filed with the court and an executor is appointed: An executor is the person you choose to manage the distribution of your property when you die according to instructions you give in your will. The executor is responsible for managing the probate process and making sure any outstanding taxes or debts get paid. The person you choose as executor should be someone responsible and trustworthy. It might be a family member or a close friend. It doesn't necessarily have to be someone you know. Some banks or financial institutions have estate settlement departments you can entrust to manage the probate process for you for a fee. They can act as your executor and hire any lawyers, appraisers, and realtors needed for the probate process.

Sample Form: File will and appoint Executor

Commonwealth of Massachusetts
The Trial Court

Suffolk _____ Division   **Probate and Family Court Department**   Docket No. __XXX__

Probate of Will With/Without Sureties

Name of Decedent __Abigail Adams__

Domicile at Death __1776 Quincy Street__   Boston
     (street and no.)   (city or town)

__Suffolk__   Date of Death __March 9, 2004__
(county)   (zip)

Name and address of Petitioner(s) __John Adams__

__1776 Quincy Street, Boston, MA__   Status __Surviving Spouse__

Heirs at law or next of kin of deceased including surviving spouse:

Name	Residence	Relationship
	(minors and incompetents must be so designated)	
John Adams	1776 Quincy Street, Boston, MA	Surviving Spouse
John Quincy Adams	same	Son
Thomas Adams	same	Son

That said deceased left a will—XXXXXXXXXX—herewith presented, wherein your petitioner(s) is/are named execut __or__
and wherein the testat__rix__ had requested that your petitioner(s) be exempt from giving surety on his/her/their bond(s).

☒ The petitioner(s) hereby certif __ies__ that a copy of this document, along with a copy of the decedent's death certificate has been sent by certified mail to the **Division of Medical Assistance, P.O. Box 15205, Worcester, Massachusetts 01615-9906.**

Wherefore your petitioner(s) pray(s) that said will—XXXXXXXXXX—may be proved and allowed, and that he/she/they be appointed execut____ thereof, with/XXXXX surety on hisXXXXX bond(s) and certif __ies__ under the penalties of perjury that the statements herein contained are true to the best of hisXXXXXXknowledge and belief.

Date__June 18, 2003__   Signature(s) __/s/ John Adams__

The undersigned hereby assent to the foregoing petition and to the allowance of the will without testimony.
__/s/ John Quincy Adams__
__/s/ Thomas Adams__

DECREE

All persons interested having been notified in accordance with the law or having assented and no objections being made thereto, it is decreed that said instrument(s) be approved and allowed as the last will and testament of said deceased, and that said petitioner(s): __John Adams__
of __Boston__
XXX _____ of _____
_____ be appointed
execut __or__ thereof, first giving bond with __out__ sureties for the due performance of said trust.

Date__June 18, 2004__   __/s/ Justice__
         Justice of the Probate and Family Court

CJ-P 2 (11/01)

If you didn't have a will, the courts will appoint someone to act as the administrator of your estate. A close relative is usually chosen to serve in this capacity.

2. Assets are collected and inventoried: The probate court will ask for a complete inventory of all the assets that will be distributed as part of your estate. This property will then be collected and held until the court authorizes the executor to distribute it.

When making your estate plan, it's important to keep a list of all of your property and to update this inventory as the years go by. It'll make it easier for the probate court and your loved ones when the time comes to distribute your assets after your death.

3. Debts and taxes are paid out of the assets: Your estate may be subject to estate taxes, which need to be paid by the executor using a portion of the estate assets. A federal estate tax return must be filed within nine months of the date of death if the estate is greater than the estate tax exemption amount (mentioned earlier). Creditors are also allowed to make claims on any unpaid debts you leave behind. It's the executor's responsibility to make sure these bills get paid.

4. Assets are distributed to beneficiaries: Whatever remains after paying the taxes and any outstanding debts is then distributed by the executor to the beneficiaries. The executor must file a final account with the probate court, which lists all expenses and distributions.

> *There are going to be some things — like furniture, clothing, jewelry, family heirlooms, and personal possessions — that may lack specific distribution instructions in your will. It's important to have some kind of written plan for making sure these possessions are passed on to loved ones fairly and equally without causing conflict or rivalries.*

What assets are subject to probate?

Any asset you own by yourself is typically subject to probate. This can be something as simple as a watch, or something much larger, like a car or a house. It can also be a less tangible thing, like an interest in a business or the copyright to a song.

With assets that are jointly owned, the ownership passes automatically to the surviving co-owner without having to be included in the probate process. A house that's jointly owned by a husband and wife will pass automatically to the wife if the husband dies, or vice versa. The same rule applies to bank accounts, cars, or any other piece of property that's jointly owned.

> *When property is joint-owned it only avoids probate if one owner survives the other. Once the surviving owner dies, the asset passes through probate.*

Sample Form: Final Account for Estate

Commonwealth of Massachusetts
The Trial Court

Suffolk __Division__   **Probate and Family Court Department**   Docket No. ___XXX___

Account

First and Final _____ Account of __John Adams__

_____ ~~and~~

_____ as __Executor of will of Abigal Adams__

(Specify type of fiduciary and name of estate)

This account is for the period of __March 9, 2004__ to __March 9, 2005__

_____ inclusive.

Principal amounts received per Schedule A $ __583,500__

Principal payments and charges per Schedule B $ __583,500__

Principal balance invested per Schedule C $ __None__

    Market value as of _____ per Schedule C $ _____
           (date)

Income received per Schedule D $ _____

Payments from income per Schedule E $ _____

Income balance per Schedule F $ _____

The United States Veterans' Administration ~~is~~ - is not - a party in interest to this account. The ward ~~is~~ - is not - a patient in a State Hospital.

I - ~~We~~ certify under the penalties of perjury that the within account is just and true.

Date __March 10, 2005__   /s/ John Adams _____

_____

_____
                          Signature of Fiduciary

The undersigned, being _____ interested, having examined the foregoing account, request that the same may be allowed without further notice.

_____

_____

_____

_____

CJ-P 30 (8/88)

Any asset that you own for which you've been named a beneficiary also transfers automatically without having to go through the probate process. Good examples of these assets would be a 401(k) retirement plan, a life insurance plan, an annuity, or a trust with a named beneficiary.

What's the difference between probate assets and assets subject to estate tax?

Just because you avoid probate doesn't mean you avoid estate taxes.

This can be confusing. There are assets that may be included in your estate for estate tax purposes but that aren't subject to probate. These would include assets put in a trust or property that is distributed directly to a named beneficiary or surviving joint owners.

> **Example 1:** Ed buys a life insurance policy and names his son as beneficiary. When he dies, his son can collect the insurance proceeds outside of probate, but the proceeds can still be taxed for estate tax purposes.

> **Example 2:** Jane creates a revocable trust for her three children. If she dies, the assets in her trust avoid probate. They pass automatically to her children but are still subject to estate tax.

What are some disadvantages of probate?

1. Costs: Probate costs money and this money is drawn directly from the assets of the estate. Fees include the cost of executor (if you go through a bank or financial service firm), attorney fees, court costs, filing fees, appraisal fees (when appraisers are hired to determine the value of property), and sales expenses (if realtors are hired to sell property). To make these fees less of a nuisance, many states have laws that cap the maximum amount of fees that can be charged.

2. Delay: Probate can be time-consuming compared to alternate methods of transfer, like passing property through a trust or naming a beneficiary. It takes time to appoint an executor or administrator, file the will with the court, and inventory the assets. It usually takes six months for a partial distribution of assets and one year before a final distribution can be made. Non-probate transfers take place as soon as the state tax release, if required, is obtained.

3. Publicity: All documents in probate court are a matter of public record and certain notices have to be published by law in the local paper. Details about your finances are publicly accessible and this can create some problems. For instance, there may be some embarrassing or private things in your records you don't want neighbors to know — like the fact that you disinherited your irresponsible son. Also, because the records are in the public domain, they can be contested. Creditors can file claims against your estate for debts left unpaid.

4. Psychological Concerns: Probate takes a long time and in many ways prolongs the sense of loss that follows closely on the heels of a loved one's death. If you don't want to force your loved ones to have to go through this process, it may be better to seek alternate ways of passing wealth.

Probate may have one advantage. It provides court supervision and court approval of your estate distribution, which adds a stamp of legitimacy to the whole affair.

Chapter 8

Wills: Your Legal Voice From Beyond the Grave

SAM SAYS:

"Don't waste anything. If it's still good, keep it." I hear that from my parents all the time. Does this hold true for wills? Many times, yes.

A will speaks for you at your death, so if your will still says what you want it to say, it's still good. So keep it!

A will communicates your desires and intentions for the distribution of your property at your death. It's a legally binding statement that names the people you want to receive your assets — your beneficiaries. The will only applies to probate property; it doesn't apply to other types of property that pass outside of probate — such as jointly held property (usually a house), trust property, and life insurance.

The requirements for a will vary from state to state. In Massachusetts, for example, you have to be at least 18 years old to create a will. The will must be in writing and signed by you as the testator — the person making the will — in the presence of two witnesses.

Other states allow less-formally executed documents to serve as a will. Some states (not Massachusetts) allow what are known as holographic wills. These wills are written and signed in the handwriting of the testator and don't require any witnesses.

Why Do I Need A Will?

Once you're dead, you're no longer available to tell people your intentions. You've lost your say in matters you'd probably be interested in if you were still alive, things like who should get your car or when your grandchildren should be eligible to receive their inheritance. These are important issues, and you want to be sure that the resolution of these questions does not cause a disruption to your family or your financial plan.

A will acts as your legal voice and literally allows you to speak and act from the grave. Most people have wills drafted by their attorneys once they have children so they can provide for them in case of death. It's not uncommon, however, for people to have wills revised or created later in life after they're retired. It's generally better to create a will when you're young and keep updating it as you get older and your property or family circumstances change.

There are several reasons why you should consider creating a will, if you haven't done so already.

Reason #1: So you can make sure your assets stay in the bloodline.

A will allows you to dispose of your property any way you want after you die. It basically allows you to select beneficiaries, or the people you want to inherit or receive your property. You can also set up something called a trust, which is a kind of holding-box that allows you to continue investing and distributing your assets to beneficiaries for as long as you want. A will can direct that your assets be placed in a trust for the benefit of your loved ones. It's like Rich's mom always says: No Blood, No Money.

Reason #2: So you can minimize tax liabilities.

Wills have provisions that allow you to take advantage of certain tax credits, such as the estate and spousal tax credits mentioned in the previous chapter. For example, if a husband leaves $3 million to be given to his wife upon his death, that $3 million can pass tax-free. Any of that $3 million she passes on to her children will be taxed. A will can be set up so that the husband passes some of the money tax-free to his wife and the rest to his children in a way that utilizes his Estate Tax Credit.

Reason #3: So you can appoint someone to administer your estate.

A will allows you to name an executor for your estate, who acts as your representative when you die. The executor is the manager of your estate. His or her job is to make sure your assets go to the right people when you die, as dictated by your will. It's often best to choose someone who won't charge money to act as your executor, such as a good friend or family member. If you do select an attorney to do the job, fees for this work will be payable from the assets of your estate. You can also provide in your will that the executor is not required to post a Fiduciary Bond during the probate process.

Reason #4: So you can designate a guardian for your children.

A will allows you to designate a legal guardian who will take care of your minor children in case you die. If you don't specify a legal guardian in your will, the court will appoint one for you. This could create delays, complications, and disputes for your family members.

Reason #5: So you can limit your probate costs and delays.

As we wrote above, before your property can be distributed to your family, it has to go through the probate court. The process can take longer and cost more if you don't have a will.

What Happens If I Die Without A Will?

We've already looked at a few of the reasons why creating a will is a good idea, but what happens if for some reason you die before you get a chance to create one for yourself?

Dying without a will is called dying intestate. If you die intestate, a couple of things can happen:

- **State laws will determine who will inherit your property and assets and how much they get.**

  Some states give half of everything to the surviving spouse and the other half to children. Some states give everything to the surviving spouse and nothing to the children. Some states give a specified amount of money to the surviving spouse, plus half the remainder of the estate to him/her. If you're unmarried and don't have children, your assets could go to the state — and who wants that?

  The laws of intestacy are complex and can lead to unintended results. In Massachusetts, for example, if a married person dies without a will and has a surviving spouse and children, half the probate assets would be distributed to the spouse and half among the children. If the married person had no children but had siblings, the surviving spouse gets the first $200,000 plus half of the remainder, and the rest is divided among the siblings. In a $1 million estate, this means the spouse would get $600,000 and the remaining $400,000 would be distributed among the siblings.

  A will could prevent these types of situations from occurring.

- **The probate court will specify a guardian for your minor children and the administrator of your estate.**

Most likely, you have very definite ideas about who should take care of your minor children if you die. If you fail to specify who you want to be the guardian of your children, the court will appoint someone it chooses. The same holds true for the executor — if you fail to state your preference, the court will appoint someone as the administrator. If you leave the decision up to the court by not specifying these things in your will, it could create disputes among your living relatives and friends.

What Goes Into A Will Anyway?

Wills have several main parts, or provisions, that have to be filled in by the testator — the person writing the will, who typically acts through an attorney.

Here are some of the provisions a will can have:

Your Legal Residence:

Your legal residence is where you live. You should specify your town, county, and state of residency. Otherwise, there could be a dispute about where to probate your will. If you own real estate outside of the state of your residency you may have to go through a second probate proceeding in order to transfer the property in the other state. For example, if you reside in Massachusetts but have a vacation home in Florida, probate proceedings would have to be initiated in both states upon your death. Twice the probate isn't necessarily twice the fun.

Your Legal Name:

This is the name used on official documents such as deeds, insurance policies, bank accounts, credit cards, and birth records. Use your formal name as it appears on your birth certificate or marriage records — Michael Franklin Black, not Mike Black. To avoid confusion, pay particular attention to using your correct legal name, especially if you've been divorced or have changed your legal name during your lifetime.

A Revocation of any Prior Wills or Codicils:

If you have executed any prior wills, or if you have amendments (codicils) to a previous will you'd like to revoke (cancel so they're no longer effective), you have to make an affirmative statement to this effect in your new will. Let's say you created a will in 1996 that leaves half your property to your spouse and the other half to your children. In 2001 you decide to make a new will to include your nieces and nephews. You'd want to have a provision in the new will to revoke the old will in its entirety. This provision makes the old will null and void.

Designation of Executor (Who's In Charge?):

The executor of the will manages the estate, collects the assets, probates the will, notifies the beneficiaries, distributes the property, and pays any taxes that are due. You can choose one or several executors. It can be a family member, a friend, a corporate fiduciary (such as a bank or trust company), or an attorney. The executor must file a bond with the probate court unless the will exempts them. Be advised that selecting a friend or relative to serve as executor is often the cheapest way to go.

Funeral Arrangements:

There's usually a provision in the will that indicates how you'd like to be buried (in the ground or cremated) and whether or not you'd like to have your organs donated. A person is usually buried long before the will goes to probate, so you should leave a copy of your burial instructions behind for your family so they understand the arrangements to make with the funeral director.

> *Baseball legend Ted Williams left specific instructions in his will to be cremated upon his death. Before the will was submitted to probate, Ted's son, John Henry, had his body cryogenically frozen somewhere in Arizona. Ted's daughter and close friends were outraged by what they saw as a blatant violation of Ted's will. Years have passed, and Ted's body still remains in deep freeze. It just goes to show that some final requests are never quite final.*

A Self-Proving Affidavit:

This is a provision added to the will that allows the will to be accepted by the probate court without the testimony of witnesses. It helps speed up the probate process. The affidavit is signed by the person making the will (testator), the witnesses, and a notary public to affirm that the document is intended to be a will and that it was properly signed and witnessed.

Debts & Taxes (Pass On The House With The Mortgage):

You can specify in your will what assets should be used to pay off any debts and taxes owed to the state. You can also specify whether the estate should pay off any mortgages or liens on real estate, or if the beneficiary should inherit the property subject to mortgage or lien. For example, if a son inherits a vacation house on Nantucket from his father, and the house has a $100,000 mortgage, the will can determine whether the son should inherit the house with the mortgage paid off by the estate, or if he should inherit the house and pay the mortgage himself.

Distribution of Assets:

As already mentioned, property owned jointly with right of survivorship or assets with a named beneficiary (e.g., life insurance) pass outside of probate. Property owned only by you or with tenants in common and assets with no named beneficiaries (e.g., a retirement plan) are all distributed according to the terms of the will — to whomever you choose, however you want. There are several methods of distributing assets.

METHODS OF DISTRIBUTING ASSETS (SO WHO GETS MOM'S RING?):

- **Specific Bequests:** These are specific gifts made to specific people — things like grandma's wedding ring, Uncle Lenny's leather sofa, Cousin Judy's painting of Aunt Sarah, my 1982 Ford Mustang, and your Neil Diamond record collection (if you have one). If you no longer own the item at the time the will gets executed, the chosen beneficiary gets nothing: this is called ademption. For example, if grandma leaves her ring to her granddaughter Jane, and in the meantime sells it to a pawn shop for quick cash, Jane won't inherit the ring when grandma dies or receive any kind of cash value.

> *Specific bequests are often left outside of the will. Usually they're made on a piece of paper that gives detailed instructions about distributing property. This memo must be referred to in the will to be legally binding. This is generally the matter of simply stating, "My personal property should be distributed according to memo dated February 12, 2004."*

- **General Bequests:** These are gifts that do not refer to any particular items. Some examples of general bequests would be $10,000, or one of my automobiles (executor gets to choose which one).

- **Residuary Estate:** This is what's left in the estate after debts, taxes, expenses, and specific and general bequests are all made. The residuary estate includes all your remaining assets waiting to be distributed. Typically you would divide this up proportionally among your family: maybe give 40% to your son, 40% to your daughter, and 20% to your favorite niece.

Will Contests or Disputes (IF YOU DON'T LIKE IT, YOU GET NOTHING):

Some wills have a no contest clause, so that if a beneficiary contests, or challenges, the will and loses that challenge in court, they'll get nothing. To prevent contests or disputes, it's often a good idea to explain the reason you distributed assets the way you did in a letter or videotape for your family. Contests can also be prevented by using trusts to distribute assets instead of the will.

What Happens if a Beneficiary Dies Before I Do? You Can Make Sure it Stays in the Bloodline!

If a beneficiary dies before the person making the will, two things can happen: either the bequest could fail and no gift is made, or under state law, also called an anti-lapse law, the property could pass to the children of the beneficiary who died. It's best to specify in the will what should happen to your assets if your beneficiary dies. Check out what the law says in the state where you live.

In Massachusetts, if the beneficiary of a will who predeceases the testator is related to the testator, the property passes to the late beneficiary's children unless the will states otherwise. If the beneficiary who predeceases the testator is not related, the bequest fails.

Durable Power of Attorney (If I Can't Act While I'm Living I Want to Make Sure I Trust the Person Who Takes My Place):

A will allows you to distribute property after death, but a special document called durable power of attorney allows you to designate someone to manage and distribute assets during your life in case you're unable to do so because you're incompetent or incapacitated through illness. Durable power of attorney gives another person "attorney-in-fact" powers. That person can do anything you can do, including access bank accounts and pay bills. Giving someone this power is often a good idea, because if you don't have durable power of attorney, your family must go to court to appoint a guardian or conservator, which can be expensive and contentious.

Why Would Someone Challenge My Will?
(Opening the Door to Complaints)

When your will passes through probate, a written announcement contain-ing details about your estate usually must be published in your local paper. Your executor must also get written signatures from your relatives for the will to be approved by the probate court. This opens up the door to dispute, and allows friends, family, or others to file an objection to the will. Don't be surprised: there are often legitimate occasions when a friend or family might challenge your will. Mostly the causes for contest are simple. There may be a written mistake on the document (maybe a missing decimal point or an extra zero somewhere) or the will might not have been executed properly. But sometimes the causes for contest are complicated and messy. A friend or family member who feels particularly short-changed by a will can claim that it was written with undue influence, which is a fancy way of saying that the testator was being pressured to distribute assets in a certain way. They can also claim that the will being presented to probate is an older ver-sion, and that a new version of the will exists. Of course, challenges don't always end in victory. They have to be decided by the court.

In granting durable power of attorney, it's a good idea to select someone who's responsible, lives close by, and is absolutely trust-worthy. The durable power of attorney can take effect immedi-ately or when you become incapacitated (this is known as "spring-ing"). If you do decide on "springing" power, make sure you spec-ify in the document how to determine if you're incapacitated. You can revoke your durable power of attorney at any time by notify-ing your "attorney in fact" in writing.

There are other ways to grant people power over your assets while you're still alive. These are called trusts, and we'll talk about them in the next chapter.

Chapter 9

Trusts: Your Bullet-Proof Box

(The Way You Can Make Sure
Your Assets Stay in the Bloodline)

RICH'S REMARKS:

"No Blood, No Money" — that's the term my mom used that was so effective I just had to use it for the title of the book. I'm not really sure if my mom actually uttered those exact words but she has made it clear on more than one occasion that when she passes on she wants her assets to go to her children and grandchildren. It's not that she doesn't care for my wife, but it's just the way she thinks.

So don't take offense to "No Blood, No Money." Just accept it as one of the wishes that should be carried out.

A trust is a legal entity that allows you to hold and manage your assets while you're alive or after you're dead. Think of it as a bullet-proof box a lawyer can create to protect your assets from certain tax liabilities and guarantee that your beneficiaries get the wealth you want them to have.

The assets that go into a trust can include any tangible, intangible, or real estate property you own. By putting these assets in a trust, you, the settlor (or person creating the trust), are basically transferring ownership to the trust itself, which holds it for your benefit or the benefit of anyone you designate. Trusts are managed by one or more trustees, who safeguard and invest the assets and make sure beneficiaries get pay-outs according to the distribution plan you set up.

Trustees can be individuals (friends or family members), or corporate fiduciaries (e.g., banks or trust companies). No matter who you choose as your trustee, he or she has a legal obligation to act for the benefit of the trust beneficiaries. In the trust document, also known as the agreement of trust, the settlor specifically designates:

- Who the trustee(s) will be and how the assets in the trust will be invested.
- Who the beneficiaries will be.
- The terms under which the money will be paid out (for example, only when the beneficiary reaches 21).
- How often money will be paid out.

The trust essentially guarantees that your assets will be invested, managed, and protected after you die and distributed according to your wishes.

Example: A grandfather puts $20,000 in trust for his eight-year-old granddaughter's college education and names Chemical Bank as the trustee. They invest the money in stocks, bonds, and mutual funds, and continue investing in these assets even after Grandpa passes away shortly before his granddaughter's 16th birthday. When the granddaughter gets accepted to Dartmouth College, she notifies Chemical Bank and they write her a check to cover her first year's tuition. According to the agreement of trust set up by her grandfather, she'll continue to receive a check every year she's at school. After she graduates, whatever remains in the trust will be given to her as a lump sum. If the granddaughter drops out of the college in her second year, she'll stop receiving checks until she turns 35. At that age, she'll receive whatever remains of the original $20,000 invested in her name.

WHY SET UP A TRUST? (WHY NOT — THERE'S NO DOWNSIDE EXCEPT PAYING THE LAWYER!)

Trusts used to be created only for the Rockefellers of the world. Now they're being used by just about anybody. There's a good reason for this.

In the old days, most people were lucky if they could retire with their mortgage paid off and a couple thousand dollars in the bank. These were assets you lived on through your retirement and passed on to your family when you died. Nowadays, many people are investing their money in assets that continue to produce interest pay-outs over time. Instead of selling these assets for cash value upon retirement, or transferring them directly to loved ones at the time of death through a will, these people have decided to keep them safe in a trust, where they can continue to collect interest for a future time when ownership is ready to be transferred. Trusts therefore offer people more control over their assets for longer periods of time, including after death. Assets held in trust also realize certain tax savings, which many people also find attractive.

Here are some reasons for setting up a trust:

Reason #1: So you can avoid probate

Assets put in a trust pass directly to the beneficiaries you determine, whenever and however you want. Even after you're dead, the trust can continue to distribute assets to the beneficiaries. In a sense, the trust outlives you. Because assets pass directly, they avoid probate, which means your estate avoids probate costs and your family and loved ones avoid the time and hassle of having to wait for the probate process to conclude. Avoiding probate also means that you avoid having to disclose information about your estate in the newspapers.

Reason #2: So you can continue to manage and invest your assets

When you set up a trust, you appoint a trustee to manage and invest your assets. You literally hand control of your assets over to that person. This comes in handy in case you suddenly become incapacitated and can no longer manage the assets yourself. It also comes in handy if you decide to provide continued professional management of your assets after you die. That way instead of transferring your assets in a lump sum to beneficiaries upon your death, you can have them build interest, which can be distributed over time. The trust therefore acts as a delay mechanism for managing and distributing wealth, whereas a will typically hands complete ownership of assets to the beneficiary all at once. Many trustees are professional money managers who work for a fiduciary company such as a bank or trust company. Their job is to invest your money in assets they think will earn interest over time without putting your wealth in too much risk. The ultimate responsibility of any trustee is to act in the best interest of your beneficiaries. You can have more than one trustee if you like.

Reason #3: So you can protect your assets (you set up the rules of the trust)

Aside from thieves, and the occasional greedy in-law, you might think that there isn't anyone else you'd like to protect your assets from. But when you put your assets in trust, you're really protecting your assets for your beneficiaries, and sometimes from your beneficiaries. You know the old expression that people are their own worst enemies? This is especially true when it comes to managing money. You may have a child, spouse, or relative who's awful with money. You know that if you hand your assets to that person all at once, the money will be gone within a month. Trusts offer a mechanism to distribute wealth over time, by giving you control over how much and under what conditions a beneficiary can receive any funds. A trust can act as a safeguard to careless spending. It can hold assets until the beneficiary reaches a more responsible age, or distribute pay-outs in small increments instead of all at once. You can also include a spendthrift clause in your trust, which allows you to keep beneficiaries' creditors from getting assets coming their way.

Reason #4: So you can qualify for Medicaid

Most states set a limit on the amount of assets you can own in order to qualify for Medicaid coverage of nursing home care. If the value of your assets total more than the required amount, you have to spend down until you reach the limit. Trusts can be used to shelter and protect assets from being spent down. Assets placed in certain types of trusts belong to the trust, not you, and therefore do not count against you when you apply for Medicaid. This is an ever-changing area of law so be careful!

Reason #5: So you can control the distribution of assets to your children ("No Blood, No Money" provisions)

Trusts allow you to distribute assets in any manner or at any time you choose. A beneficiary may have to wait one month to receive assets from your trust, or they may have to wait 20 years. The timing is up to you. This control feature of trusts is particularly useful if you have minor children who would not be ready to inherit large sums of money if you pass away. A trust allows you to hold out on distribution of assets until minors reach an adult age, such as 18 or 21, or until there's an occasion when the money will be useful to them, such as paying for college or buying their first home.

Reason #6: So you can provide for dependent family members (How to take care of Mom without risking principal)

A trust protects and manages assets that can be used to take care of dependent parents or other family members in case of sudden death. For example, a son can set aside $10,000 in trust to be distributed to his 72-year old mother. When the mother dies, the trust can be set up so that the remainder can be given to his children. A trust can also be used to provide for non-blood related dependents or family members. For example, a generous father can leave $5,000 to the son-in-law of his deceased daughter.

Reason #7: So you can maximize tax savings (After you make it and save it, make sure you keep it!)

A trust can be used to realize tax savings. For example, if you're married and the value of your estate adds up to more than the Estate Tax Credit amount ($2 million for 2006, 2007, and 2008), married couples can create what's known as a "credit shelter trust" to protect assets from Federal Estate Taxes. Trusts can also be used to protect life insurance policies from estate taxes as well.

WHAT ARE THE COMMON TYPES OF TRUSTS?

Trusts can come in all shapes and sizes, but here are some of the most common forms of trusts:

Testamentary Trusts (WHEN YOU NEED THE COURTS TO MAKE SURE YOUR WISHES ARE CARRIED OUT)

A testamentary trust is a type of trust established in the will. It comes into existence when the will is probated and continues after probate is completed. One benefit of a testamentary trust is the low administrative cost. Costs are low because the trust isn't funded until after your death, which means you don't have to pay someone to manage and invest your trust's funds while you're still alive.

Testamentary trusts, however, don't protect your estate from probate, which is a big disadvantage for some people.

Living Trusts (You set it up while living)

A living trust, sometimes called an "inter vivos" trust, is a trust created during your life. Unlike a testamentary trust, it can be funded while you're still alive. When you create a living trust, you basically transfer ownership of your assets to the trust. The assets are managed by a trustee on behalf of its named beneficiaries. Because the assets are put in trust, they don't count as part of your probate estate, and therefore avoid probate.

There are two types of living trusts: revocable and irrevocable.

Revocable Trust (You are the trustee and beneficiary)

A revocable living trust gives you flexibility and control. It allows you to revoke, amend, spend, or take back whatever you put into the trust. Assets placed in revocable trust avoid probate and pass directly to beneficiaries. The trust can receive assets from your estate using a pour over will. However, since you maintain control of the assets, and can take them out of the trust, they're included in your estate for estate tax purposes.

Tax Liabilities

Some types of assets trigger adverse tax consequences when transferred to a revocable trust, such as:

- **S Corporation Stock:** A small, closely held company could lose S Corporation status, which allows income and losses to pass through to shareholders.

- **Stock Options:** Putting stock options in trust could trigger a taxable gain.
- **IRAs & Pension Plans:** Assets placed in IRAs and pension plans could trigger tax liabilities when placed in a revocable trust. This is a very complex area that may require the consultation of a professional planner.
- **Real Estate:** Transferring real estate into trust could trigger state transfer taxes. You could also lose your Homestead Exemption, which protects your house from creditors.

Credit Shelter Trust (Tax Advantages For Married Couples)

Remember that the marital deduction allows you to leave any or all of your estate to your surviving spouse free from any federal estate tax. This may sound like a good deal, but actually it can be a tax trap depending on the amount of assets your surviving spouse owns at the time of his or her death. The marital deduction only defers estate taxes, it doesn't eliminate or reduce them. When your surviving spouse eventually dies, all of your remaining assets will be subject to estate taxes.

To save on estate taxes, you can use a type of revocable living trust called a "credit shelter" or "by-pass trust." Instead of giving all the assets to your surviving spouse outright, the credit shelter trust shelters your assets and allows an amount equal to the estate tax credit to by-pass the estate tax. The credit shelter trust can be used if your combined estate as a couple exceeds the estate tax credit amount of $2 million for 2006, 2007, and 2008.

Example:
Suppose Jack and Diane are married and have the following assets:

House	$1.1 million
Bank Accounts	$200,000
Stocks	$500,000
Bonds	$800,000
Life Insurance	$1 million
Annuities	$800,000
Total	$4.4 Million

Scenario 1: Tax Savings With Marital Deduction Only — Everything Goes To Surviving Spouse

Suppose Jack died in 2006 and in a simple will left everything ($4.4 million) to his wife Diane. Because of the marital deduction, there's no estate tax due upon Jack's death, which means that the entire $4.4 million passes to Diane tax-free. If Diane passes away a year later in 2007, the remainder of Jack's estate is subject to estate taxes minus whatever amount can be deducted as part of Diane's estate tax credit ($2 million in 2006). In the end, 25% of Jack's original $4.4 million (about $1.1 million) gets claimed in taxes, which leaves Jack and Diane's children, Clair and Nelson, with a measly $3,296,000 in inheritance.

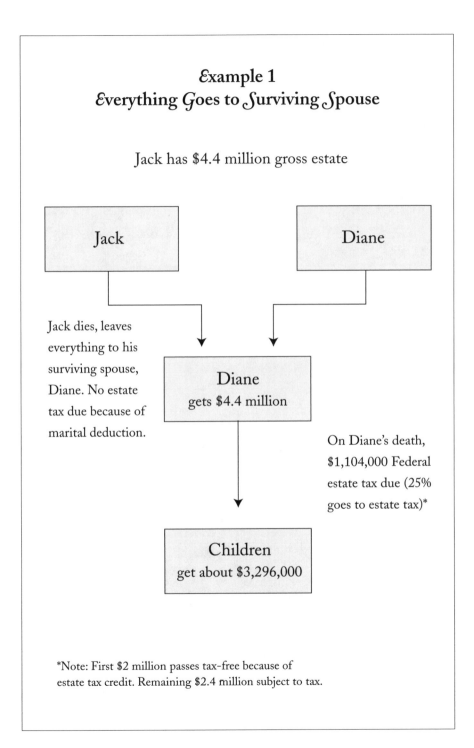

Example 1
Everything Goes to Surviving Spouse

Jack has $4.4 million gross estate

Jack

Diane

Jack dies, leaves everything to his surviving spouse, Diane. No estate tax due because of marital deduction.

Diane
gets $4.4 million

On Diane's death, $1,104,000 Federal estate tax due (25% goes to estate tax)*

Children
get about $3,296,000

*Note: First $2 million passes tax-free because of estate tax credit. Remaining $2.4 million subject to tax.

Scenario 2: Tax Savings With Credit Shelter Trust

Suppose Jack created a Credit Shelter Trust and named his wife Diane as the initial beneficiary. On Jack's death in 2006, his will directed that $2 million of his assets be put in the trust. When Jack died, $2.4 million passed tax-free to Diane because of the marital deduction. The $2 million he put in trust also passed tax-free since the estate tax credit amount in 2006 was $2 million. When Diane dies in 2007, only $2.4 million of Jack's estate is subject to taxes. The other $2 million remains sheltered and passes directly to Clair and Nelson.

The credit shelter trust reduced Jack's estate taxes from 25% to 4%. In the long run, only $184,000 will be lost in taxes. Clair and Nelson's inheritance will be greatly increased.

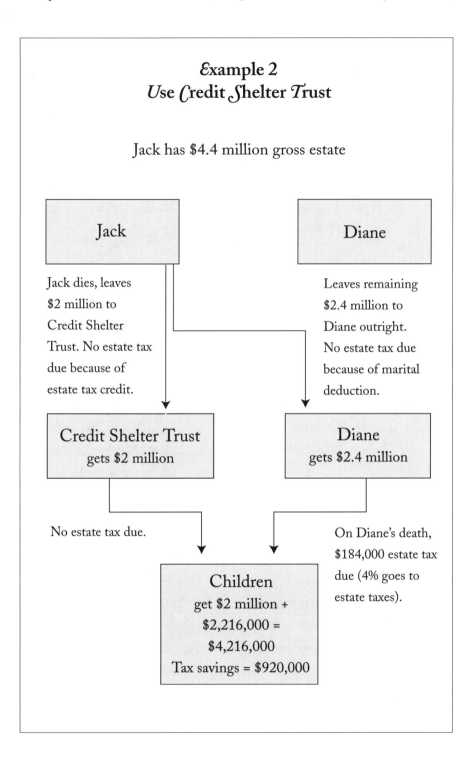

Example 2
Use Credit Shelter Trust

Jack has $4.4 million gross estate

Jack

Diane

Jack dies, leaves $2 million to Credit Shelter Trust. No estate tax due because of estate tax credit.

Leaves remaining $2.4 million to Diane outright. No estate tax due because of marital deduction.

Credit Shelter Trust
gets $2 million

Diane
gets $2.4 million

No estate tax due.

On Diane's death, $184,000 estate tax due (4% goes to estate taxes).

Children
get $2 million + $2,216,000 = $4,216,000
Tax savings = $920,000

Credit Shelter Trust Provisions

The Credit Shelter Trust is typically set up as a revocable living trust. It's created during life and usually funded at death, using a pour-over will. An amount equal to the maximum estate tax credit can be sheltered by the trust, which in 2006 is $2 million.

Your surviving spouse can't have unfettered access to the trust principal, otherwise it would be included in his or her estate. He or she can have access to the following, though:

• **Income from the trust for life:** This includes any income the assets are earning in terms of interest, dividends, proceeds from sales, etc.

• **Limited right to withdraw principle:** The surviving spouse's rights are limited to what's known as an "ascertainable standard." This means they can use assets to cover the cost of health, education, and the financial support of family members and dependents. They can have the right to withdraw each year the greater of $5,000 or 5% of the value of the trust assets for any purpose. They can also have the right to use trust assets to make gifts to others, including children and grandchildren.

When both spouses die, the remaining assets in a credit shelter trust go to the surviving beneficiaries (in the example of Jack and Diane, the surviving beneficiaries are their children Clair and Nelson). The assets in the trust, including any increase in value, won't be included in the surviving spouse's estate, and therefore aren't subject to estate tax on the surviving spouse's death.

Irrevocable Trust (Once It's Gone, You Can't Take It Back)

The provisions of an irrevocable trust are fixed. Property or assets can't be removed and the terms can't change. This type of trust is usually created to save on federal estate taxes. Because the assets in an irrevocable trust can't be taken back, they're no longer included as part of the estate and aren't subject to estate taxes. However, assets placed in irrevocable trust are still subject to gift tax.

An irrevocable trust can't be amended, altered, or terminated by the person who created the trust. You can't take back assets the way you can with a revocable trust. Irrevocable trusts are mostly useful when you want to make a gift to a spouse or beneficiary final and complete, thereby avoiding estate taxes. Irrevocable trusts are commonly used for transferring appreciating assets, as well as life insurance. They can also be used with real estate while the donor retains a life estate.

The downside of an irrevocable trust is that you lose direct control of the assets. These trusts also tend to cost more to manage and can result in gift tax liabilities at the time of transfer.

Life Insurance and Irrevocable Trusts (Pass It On Without Paying Estate Taxes)

You can realize huge estate tax savings by transferring a life insurance policy into an irrevocable trust. This type of trust is called an "ILIT", which stands for irrevocable life insurance trust.

In a nutshell, an ILIT allows you to take proceeds from your life insurance policy completely out of the estate for estate tax purposes. It also allows you to provide management of proceeds from the life insurance policy on your death.

> *If you die within three years of transferring a life insurance policy into a trust, the proceeds of the policy can be included in your taxable estate.*

There are two ways to create an ILIT trust: you can transfer your life insurance policy into the trust or have the trustee purchase a life insurance policy in your name. As the settlor, you make cash gifts over time to pay the life insurance premiums. The gift tax on the policy is based on the value at time of transfer, which is very low compared to the value of the policy at the time of death. You can use the $12,000 annual gift tax exemption when you pay the premium.

Example: Tax Savings From an ILIT

Let's go back to Jack and Diane. Suppose Jack put his $1 million life insurance policy into an ILIT in 2000 and $2 million in a Credit Shelter Trust when he passed away in 2006. The remaining $1.4 million in assets passed tax-free to his wife Diane because of the marital deduction. What happens to Jack's estate in this scenario, after his death?

In short, the beneficiaries, Clair and Nelson, inherit the entire estate without losing a dime in estate taxes:

- $2 million passes tax-free because of the Credit Shelter Trust.
- $1 million passes tax-free because of the ILIT.
- $1.4 million passed to Diane tax-free because of the marital deduction then passes tax-free to Clair and Nelson because of Diane's estate tax credit.

By using a combination of the ILIT and Credit Shelter Trust, Jack went from losing 25% of his estate in taxes to losing nothing at all. As a result, Clair and Nelson were able to inherit the full $4.4 million tax-free.

The point here is simple: if Jack is able to save that much on estate taxes, just imagine what you could save using the right combination of irrevocable and revocable trusts.

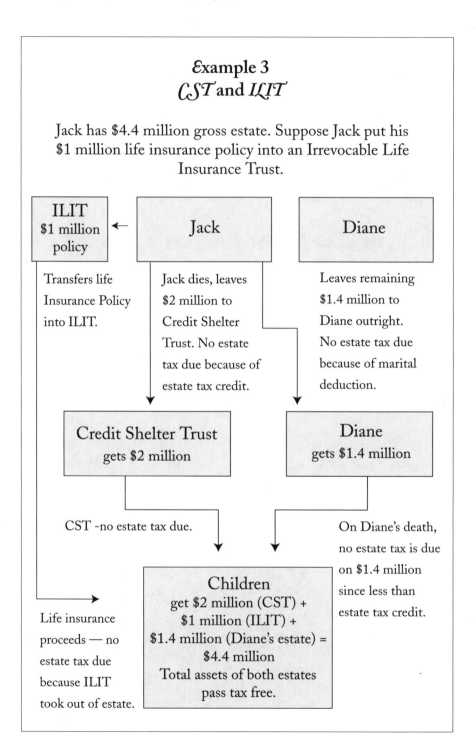

Example 3
CST and ILIT

Jack has $4.4 million gross estate. Suppose Jack put his $1 million life insurance policy into an Irrevocable Life Insurance Trust.

ILIT
$1 million policy

Jack

Diane

Transfers life Insurance Policy into ILIT.

Jack dies, leaves $2 million to Credit Shelter Trust. No estate tax due because of estate tax credit.

Leaves remaining $1.4 million to Diane outright. No estate tax due because of marital deduction.

Credit Shelter Trust
gets $2 million

Diane
gets $1.4 million

CST -no estate tax due.

On Diane's death, no estate tax is due on $1.4 million since less than estate tax credit.

Life insurance proceeds — no estate tax due because ILIT took out of estate.

Children
get $2 million (CST) + $1 million (ILIT) + $1.4 million (Diane's estate) = $4.4 million
Total assets of both estates pass tax free.

Chapter 10

Trustees & Beneficiaries:

(The Ones Who Write the Checks and the Ones Who Cash Them In)

SAM ASKS:

So, who do you trust? Is it your oldest child, smartest child, most successful child...? Just who do you want in charge if it can't be you? If you were the trustee, you'd know what to do.

The most appropriate person to appoint trustee of your trust is usually the one who thinks the most like you — the child who can step back and ask "What would Mom and Dad do in this situation?" The one who can withstand outside pressure from his or her parent or siblings, who is mentally tough. That's who your trustee should be.

C hoosing the right trustee for your trust is extremely important. The trustee is responsible for managing and investing trust assets, maintaining accounting records, filing tax returns for the trust, and distributing assets to the beneficiaries. A bad trustee can lead to increased expenses, taxes, and investment losses. A good trustee can make life easier for your family and friends by taking care of any legal or tax issues associated with the trust, and in some cases by making successful investments on their behalf.

In selecting a trustee, most people choose between a responsible friend or family member or a professional trustee (e.g., a bank, trust company, or attorney). Some people feel most comfortable with a combination of both.

WHAT KIND OF TRUSTEE SHOULD YOU CHOOSE?

Generally, the type of trustee you pick depends on a few different factors:

The Purpose of Your Trust

What's your purpose in setting up a trust? Is it simply to avoid probate? If it is, then you can set up a revocable trust and name yourself as trustee. This will allow you to manage your own assets without having to name a professional trustee. It will also allow you to select a professional or family member to serve as a back-up trustee in the event of your death.

If you want your trust to manage large sums of money for your children and grandchildren, you may want to consider choosing a professional trustee — someone who knows how to invest and protect assets over time. If you have trouble trusting total strangers with your money, you can always name a friend or family member as co-trustee.

Fees

It may be expensive to have a professional trustee manage your trust, especially if it's small. Keep in mind that some professional trustees have a minimum annual fee schedule, which could be several thousand dollars. They typically charge a percent of the total assets being managed by the trust, and often require a minimum of $500,000 to $1 million in assets under management. Professional trustees may also have additional fees for real estate management and distribution of trust assets to the beneficiaries.

If you only have $20,000 in your trust, for example, professional management fees could cost you as much as $1,000 per year. In this situation, naming a professional trustee to manage the trust hardly seems worth it. Because of the expense of hiring a professional, you might consider using more than one trustee, such as a child and a friend, and instruct them to hire professionals to manage the trust funds.

The Duration of Your Trust

How long is the trust going to last? If you're creating it for your grandchildren, it could last a long time. Naming yourself as trustee doesn't make sense unless you name someone else to serve as co-trustee. Also keep in mind that institutions generally outlive people. Chemical Bank, founded in 1916, will probably be around at least another 30 or 40 years to manage the trust for your grandchildren. Cousin Arnie, born in 1916, will be lucky to survive three or four more years and is probably not a good choice. In naming a trustee for a longer-term trust, it's generally better to select professional trustees who work for established financial institutions.

Type of Assets in the Trust

Stocks, bonds, and CDs are relatively simple forms of investments. Assets like businesses and commercial real estate are much more complicated and may require the specialized knowledge of professional managers.

Location of Assets

Where are the assets that you're putting in the trust located? Stocks, bonds, and bank accounts can typically be managed online or over the phone. Real estate is different. If you're including the apartment building you own in Boston in the trust, it doesn't make much sense to name your brother in Seattle as trustee. How's he going to make sure the building is being properly managed unless he hires someone else to do it for him?

Taxes

If you're the settlor and name yourself as trustee, you could make the trust subject to estate taxes, even if the trust is irrevocable. Naming someone else to act as trustee can limit your estate tax liability and be a good estate planning tool. Check with your professional advisors as you select your trustee to make sure you're not doing something with unintended consequences.

Trustee Pros & Cons

Here are some of the pro and con scenarios for each of the possible trustee types you can name. Keep in mind that most trusts allow for a combination of one or more trustee types.

The Settlor (You) Let's assume you name yourself as the initial trustee of your trust. There are a couple of benefits you'll enjoy. First of all, your trust will avoid probate, which means that after your death your assets will go directly to your beneficiaries. Second, you'll maintain total control over your assets while you're alive, which means you can invest them any way you want.

Of course, there are disadvantages as well. First of all, your trust won't save on estate taxes because the assets you put in trust are includable in your taxable estate. Second, your assets won't be protected from creditors because you still have access to them in trust. Finally, you may not be qualified or able to manage the assets in your trust.

Most individuals choose themselves as trustees of their revocable trusts and have a successor trustee named to take over after their death.

Family or Friends If you choose your spouse, your children, a friend, or in-law to act as trustees, co-trustees, or successor trustees, you'll benefit from the knowledge that your assets have been placed in familiar hands. Most likely your friends and family will understand how you want your assets invested and distributed. You'll be more comfortable dealing with them rather than a stranger, and their services will cost significantly less than hiring a professional trustee, if anything at all.

Of course, if you choose a family member or friend who has no background in investing or tax planning, that could be a problem. Your Uncle Eddie may be the best car salesman in Boston, but he may know absolutely nothing about annuities, stocks, or bonds. His lack of experience may wind up costing your trust money. But even if Uncle Eddie is a Wall Street wizard, he's only human, which means in essence that someday he'll die and the management of your trust assets will once again be up for grabs.

There's another major disadvantage to having a friend or family member act as your trustee: emotional conflict. Suppose you name your brother Ernie as trustee and he doesn't get along with your wife. Who's going to act as an objective intermediary when a disagreement erupts over distribution? The best trustees are often the most impartial. Keep in mind that family and friends typically play favorites.

Again consider multiple trustees so they can act as a group. Make sure there are tie-breaking rules inside the trust.

Professional Trustees If all else fails, there's one more place to go. To a professional. There are four variations of professional trustees you can turn to for help.

- **Corporate Trustees:** These are typically banks or other financial institutions with specialized trust departments. These institutions have experienced staffs that can handle both the bookkeeping and investing aspects of managing the trust. A trust officer is usually assigned to the trust so you know with whom you are dealing at all times.

If you choose a corporate trustee to manage your trust, you'll benefit from having your assets properly invested. But experience and skill offered by professional management come at a cost. Corporate trustees often charge minimum fees for managing your trust. They often lack personal knowledge of you and your family and aren't as adept at understanding the family history impacting the decisions you've made about distributions. Because they're corporate entities, they experience all the ups and downs of business — from employee turnover to corporate acquisition and relocation. The trust officer handling your trust today may resign tomorrow and relocate to the West Coast. At any time, your trust department may be bought out and moved to Chicago, which might make it harder for them to keep close tabs on assets such as real estate.

- **Investment Adviser:** Having an investment advisor act as trustee is especially helpful if the majority of trust assets are in the form of cash or securities (i.e., stocks, bonds, mutual funds). Most investment advisors are proficient in investing and will take the needs of your beneficiaries into account. Be aware, however, that some investment advisors receive commissions for investing in certain assets. This creates a potential conflict of interest that can steer some investment advisors towards investments you might have avoided during your lifetime.

- **Lawyer:** Some people choose their family lawyer(s) to serve as trustee. They're trustworthy, safe, and for the most part familiar with the beneficiaries named in the trust. Lawyers have standards of professional conduct, which keep them accountable for their actions and decisions. They may not be experts on investing, but they can select an investment advisor to invest assets and act as their advisor if need be. Some state ethics rules don't allow the attorney who drafted the trust agreement to serve as trustee because of potential conflict of interest and undue influence. You may need to hire a separate attorney to create the trust and another to serve as trustee.

Combination There's no reason why you can't have family members, friends, and professional trustees share the responsibilities of managing your trust by acting as co-trustees. This is especially beneficial if your trust has sufficient assets. A corporate trustee can manage the assets and bookkeeping. A family member can make sure beneficiaries are being taken care of sufficiently and act as a replacement trustee when a bank or corporate trustee gets bought out or moves away.

Situs (Giving Your Trust a Home)

"Situs" is a term that refers to the location of your trust, the state designated as the home of your trust. It's typically the same state as the one in which you currently live, but there may be circumstances where you want the trust to be located in another state in order to take advantage of trust laws. You can usually do this by selecting a trustee from that state.

Here are two reasons you might consider designating the situs of your trust in another state:

• **Creditor protection:** Some states, such as Alaska, offer more protection from a settlor's creditors.

• **Duration of the trust:** Most states limit the duration of trusts to 90 years. This is known as the "rule against perpetuities." But some states allow trusts (commonly known as "dynasty trusts") to continue in perpetuity, or forever. In Massachusetts, trusts of 90 years or less are presumed valid.

TRUSTEE PITFALLS (KEEP A CLOSE EYE ON YOUR MONEY)

Trustees are faced with an awesome amount of responsibility. As noted earlier, the trustee's key function is to manage the assets held in trust for the beneficiaries. This includes protecting the assets (e.g., making sure a house held in trust is properly insured), making sure the trust's assets are invested in the beneficiaries' best interest (e.g., avoiding risky investments), and making sure that the proper tax returns are filed for the trust.

Trustees have what's known as a "fiduciary duty," which means they have a legal obligation to act for the benefit of the trust and its beneficiaries, not their own. In some cases, if a trustee's action or inaction causes beneficiaries to lose money, the trustee can be held liable.

There are some things a trustee's fiduciary responsibility restricts him or her from doing:

1. The trustee can't profit personally from investments or engage in self-dealing with the trusts. For example, the trustee can't sell a painting worth $5,000 to the trust for $50,000.

2. The trustee can't mingle personal assets with trust assets. For example, the trustee shouldn't use his personal checking account as the trust's checking account.

3. The trustee can't favor one beneficiary over another. The trustee must at all times treat the beneficiaries fairly and impartially.

4. The trustee can't make investments that will jeopardize the long-term performance of the trust principal. When investing trust assets, the trustee must follow the "prudent man" rule, which means that the trustee has to use the care and judgment other prudent investors use. The trustee is ultimately judged by his or her conduct, not investment performance. For this reason, most trustees avoid speculation, day trading, and investing in unknown companies.

Being a trustee is often more complex than being the executor of a will. An executor merely collects assets in the estate and distributes them to the right people. The trustee, on the other hand, manages assets for the long haul, while also balancing the financial interests of the beneficiaries. When it comes to investing assets for beneficiaries, trustees must look at the bigger picture. Are they investing assets for children or grandchildren who will need money for their college education? Or are they investing assets for older or elderly beneficiaries who need income to live on? These are the types of considerations every trustee needs to keep in mind.

The Beneficiaries (YOUR BLOODLINE SUCCESSORS)

Life is easy for the beneficiaries. For the most part, all they should have to do is sit back, relax, and cash the checks that keep coming to them in the mail.

A beneficiary is anyone who receives distributions of money or other assets from the trust. Individuals, charities, corporations, and government entities can be named as beneficiaries of a trust. Wealthy people often leave money in their trust for foundations or land to be used for a park or nature preserve.

The trust can provide flexibility by specifying a class of beneficiaries instead of individuals. For example, some trusts leave instructions for assets to be distributed to "My children" or "My grandchildren." Naming beneficiaries by class allows you to distribute assets to those individuals or family members not yet born. These classes should be broad, but not ambiguous. Instructing a trust to distribute assets to "my relatives" is a sure-fire way to leave everyone in your family scratching their heads and fighting for every dime.

Beneficiary Interests (WHO'S GETTING WHAT TODAY AND WHO'S GETTING WHAT TOMORROW)

Principal consists of assets put in trust at the time the trust was created plus capital gains from the sale of trust assets. Income is earned by the principal in the form of interest and dividends. The trust can direct principal and income to be divided among ben-eficiaries. For example, you can direct your trust to pay income to your spouse for life, and on your spouse's death direct the remain-ing principal to be divided among your children. In that situation, your spouse has what's known as the "current interest" and your children have "future interest." Your spouse gets income now, and your children get their share or interest later. Beneficiaries with current interest usually have greater rights in the trust than those with future interests. This means that their needs get served first by the trust.

Types of Distributions: Mandatory vs. Discretionary

How much do you trust your trustee? Enough to let him distribute assets in any amount he wants to your beneficiaries? You have that option if you'd like.

There are two types of distribution methods you can instruct your trustee to follow: mandatory distribution and discretionary distribution.

Mandatory distribution directs the trustee to distribute assets as stipulated by the trust. If your trust says that income is to be provided to your spouse for life, your trustee must guarantee that happens.

Discretionary distribution gives your trustee discretion over the payment of income, principal, or both. You can vary the level of discretion by directing the trustee to distribute assets for "the support and maintenance" of your spouse or by giving the trustee complete control over how assets are distributed.

What if my lazy son is a spendthrift?

A lot of trusts are created with a "spendthrift clause" to protect trust assets from your beneficiaries' creditors. By giving your trustees discretion over distributions, you can enable them to withhold money from beneficiaries who are in debt, which also protects your assets greatly. A spendthrift clause allows you to protect trust assets in case of bankruptcy or divorce. It also allows you to protect assets on the behalf of sons, daughters, and grandkids who have compulsive spending habits.

Trust Accounting (FINANCIAL REPORTING TO KEEP EVERYONE IN THE KNOW)

Trustees are obligated by their fiduciary duty to provide account records and trust information to the beneficiaries. This is part of their central responsibility to protect the beneficiaries' interests.

In most cases, the trustee is required to provide beneficiaries with a trust account once every year, either by law or by the terms of the trust. The trustee must account for the following:

- Assets put in trust (principal)
- Taxes and expenses paid
- Assets sold or purchased
- Income earned on principal
- Distributions to beneficiaries

If the trustee refuses to provide accounting information, the beneficiaries can take him or her to court and demand that records be produced. The beneficiaries can also take the trustee to court if he or she violates his or her fiduciary duty through unnecessary expenses, theft, or self-dealing. It's usually best to consult an attorney in these situations.

Chapter 11

Long-Term Care & Medicaid Planning:
(Strategic Planning For Nursing Home Care)

RICH'S REMARKS:

You know you need money for the rest of your life. You know someday you'll die. You just don't know when or what condition you'll be in. Long-term care is the real wildcard in estate planning.

The laws and strategies are changing all the time in this area.

This is where the question of Long-Term Care Insurance comes in. If you can't get it or don't want it, there's only one other strategy: don't own anything. If you don't have it, the government can't get it.

That may be easier said than done, but there are ways you can enjoy your assets WITHOUT owning them.

T he fastest growing segment of the population is adults 85 and older. Currently, 13% of the population is comprised of older adults. By 2020, when the majority of Baby Boomers are over 65, one-fifth of Americans will be senior citizens.

The good news is: people are living longer. The bad news is: living longer comes at a price few older Americans ever expected they'd have to pay.

In terms of long-term care, the physical and mental decline that comes with getting older often leaves people dependent on others. Many elderly adults need help with everyday activities. In the old days, long-term care was provided mostly by family and friends. As more and more Americans struggle to maintain busy work and family lives of their own, providing for elderly loved ones is becoming an increasingly difficult task. Although most seniors would prefer to stay in their homes, nursing homes and other long-term care centers offer the kind of professional round-the-clock care few friends and family members can match.

Currently in the U.S. there are about 18,000 nursing homes with over 1.6 million residents. Half of all nursing home residents are age 85 and up[1]. Most residents suffer from serious illnesses and injuries that require constant medical care. Cancer, strokes, Alzheimer's, injuries due to falls, and arthritis are some of the leading causes for nursing home care.

---

[1] Centers for Disease Control and Prevention; National Center for Health Statistics: http://www.cdc.gov/nchs/fastats/nursingh.htm

The cost of nursing home care is very expensive, coming in at between $40,000 and $100,000 a year, depending on the location and level of care. Most people pay for nursing homes with their savings until their savings run out. Then they can qualify for Medicaid, which is a government assistance program that steps in.

WHAT IS MEDICAID?

Medicaid (called MassHealth in Massachusetts) is a joint federal/state program that provides medical assistance to children, seniors, and disabled persons who meet income and asset requirements. It's a means-tested program limited only to those with financial need. Medicaid covers long-term and nursing home care for those who qualify.

Medicaid covers more than half of all nursing home residents. It's become like an insurance policy for middle-class families after they exhaust their own resources. The earlier you can qualify for Medicaid, the more assets you can pass on to your family.

Medicare, which provides health coverage for those over 65, covers 100 days of nursing home care. After 100 days residents have to fend for themselves or depend on support from Medicaid.

How Do I qualify for Medicaid?

Medicaid is not for everyone. In fact, there are certain guidelines and restrictions that govern who can be considered qualified to receive it. These guidelines pertain to several areas of your wealth: your assets, your income, your estate, and your property. Many of the federal guidelines are undergoing significant changes as a result of the Deficit Reduction Act of 2005 that President Bush signed into law on February 8, 2006. States such as Massachusetts will have to bring their Medicaid programs into compliance with the new federal laws. As a result, how the changes in the Deficit Reduction Act of 2005 will be interpreted and applied can not be fully known as of this writing. Therefore, it is extremely important to have professional guidance to navigate the new and complex Medicaid eligibility rules, which are summarized below.

Asset Guidelines

To qualify for Medicaid you can't have more than $2,000 in "countable" assets. This changes slightly if you're married. The spouse of a nursing home resident (called a "community spouse" or "healthy spouse") can keep half of the couple's joint assets up to $99,540 in 2006. Some states, including Massachusetts, allow the healthy spouse to keep up to $99,540 regardless of whether or not that equals half of the combined assets.

All assets count towards Medicaid limits unless they're considered "non-countable" assets. Examples of non-countable assets include:

1. **Personal property:** Your clothing, jewelry, paintings, and baseball card collections.

2. **Automobiles:** An automobile worth $4,500 or less is considered non-countable if you're single. Your healthy spouse is allowed to

own a car of any value without it counting towards Medicaid asset limits.

3. Principal residence: Your house. It must be in the same state in which you apply for Medicaid. Under the Deficit Reduction Act of 2005, your house is not countable as long as your home equity is less than $500,000. However, if you have home equity greater than $500,000 you will not be eligible for Medicaid (the "Valuable House" rule) unless a spouse, minor or disabled child lives in the house. Any equity above the $500,000 limit is countable and considered available to pay your nursing home costs. States have the option of increasing the home equity exemption to $750,000. Some states also require you to prove that there's a reasonable possibility that you'll return home to exempt your house. Other states, such as Massachusetts, won't count the principal residence if you simply "intend" to return home. Your spouse is allowed to live in the home while you're away at a nursing home regardless of your home equity.

4. Prepaid funerals: You've heard of prepaid calling cards. Well, there are prepaid funerals as well. These don't count against Medicaid qualification.

5. Assets that are "inaccessible": Assets placed in an irrevocable trust are an example. Because the assets don't technically belong to you (they belong to the trust) they can't count against your Medicaid coverage, which is another reason why some people like irrevocable trusts. But there is a "look back" period.

Assets that fall into the above categories will not count against the $2,000 limit for single Medicaid applicants or the $99,540 spousal allowance.

But what if your countable assets exceed the Medicaid limit? You can still qualify for Medicaid, but not right away. You have to "spend down" your assets until they reach the limits. Don't let the language fool you. Spending down doesn't mean you have to go on a seven-day shopping spree on 5th Avenue, or test your luck with the slot machines in Las Vegas. It simply means that you have to pay as much as you can to the nursing home before the government takes over.

> The Medicaid program has both federal and state regulations. Since each state can have additional rules, it's important to consult a financial planner or attorney who's familiar with the regulations in your state.

Example 1: The Married Couple
Let's suppose that Tony and Carmella have a house worth $800,000 and stocks worth $180,000. When Tony goes into a nursing home after falling down the stairs, his $800,000 house does not count against his Medicaid eligibility (even though it is worth more than $500,000) because his wife, Carmella, is still living there. But half of the $180,000 he owns jointly with his wife does count. He has to spend down (i.e., pay the nursing home) about $90,000 worth of his assets before he can be considered eligible for Medicaid.

Example 2: The Single Person

Carmine is single and has a home worth $400,000 and stocks worth $180,000. He suffers a stroke. After caring for him for several months, his children decide to put him in a nursing home, with the intention that he'll one day come home. Carmine has to spend $178,000 dollars on his nursing home care so that he reaches the $2,000 asset limit before Medicaid kicks in. Because he intends to return home and his home equity is less than $500,000, however, his house is considered a non-countable asset and doesn't impact his eligibility. But beware of "estate recovery".

Example 3: The Single Person with a "Valuable House"

Maria is single and has a home worth $700,000 that she owns outright. If she suffers a stroke and ends up in a nursing home, she will not be eligible for Medicaid because her home equity exceeds $500,000. If her state decides to increase the home equity exemption to $750,000, her home would not count and she would be eligible.

Why Can't I Just Give My Assets Away?

The Medicaid program has both federal and state regulations. Since each state can have additional rules, it's important to consult a financial planner or attorney who's familiar with the regulations in your state. Medicaid imposes a penalty for transferring assets to friends and families. The reason for this is simple: Congress doesn't want people to be able to go into a nursing home one day, give away their assets the next, and then become eligible for Medicaid. The government would lose a lot of money if that happened. They're already losing enough as it is. That's why they created and recently enhanced the Medicaid transfer penalty.

The Medicaid transfer penalty will affect you if you transfer assets for less than their fair-market value (giving them away for free or close to it). The transfer penalty period covers the time in which you will be ineligible for Medicaid. The penalty is calculated by dividing the value of assets you transfer by the average monthly nursing home cost in your state.

> **Example 1:** The Price of Giving It Away
> Tony thinks he can outsmart the system. His nursing home care costs $7,000 a month, but he doesn't want to pay for it out-of-pocket. When he goes into the nursing home and applies for Medicaid, he transfers all $105,000 of his assets to his kids. As a result however, he is ineligible for Medicaid for the transfer penalty period of 15 months ($105,000/$7,000 month=15 months). In the end, he still has to pay the same amount ($105,000) out-of-pocket.

What if I transferred my vacation home or other assets to my kid six years ago? Does that free me from the penalty period?

Under the Deficit Reduction Act of 2005, Medicaid looks at all transfers (including to trusts) made within 60 months (five years) of filing an application to qualify for Medicaid. This is known as "the look-back period." Transfers made outside the look-back period will not impact Medicaid eligibility. Thus, if you transferred your vacation home to your son or daughter six years ago, you will not be subject to the transfer penalty period.

Another important provision of the new Medicaid rules concerns the transfer penalty start date. The transfer penalty does not start until you have moved into a nursing home, spent down your assets (to $2,000), and filed a Medicaid application. Since the transfer penalty does not start until after your assets are gone and you apply for Medicaid, you could be left in a dire situation where you are unable to pay for your care or qualify for Medicaid.

> **Example 2:** The Hidden Price of the Grandchildren's Tuition
> Bob transfers $98,000 to his grandchildren in 2005 to help pay for college tuition. In 2008, he is diagnosed with Alzheimer's disease and enters a nursing home. After spending down his remaining assets to $2,000 on his nursing home care, Bob applies for Medicaid in June 2009. His nursing home care costs $7,000 a month. Since the transfer to his grandchildren occurred within the five year look-back period, he is ineligible for Medicaid for the penalty period of 14 months from the date of his application in June 2009 ($98,000/$7,000 month=14 months). Medicaid will not pay the nursing home for those 14 months and Bob will have to reapply for Medicaid at the end of the penalty period.

The new Medicaid rules require each state to create a "hardship waiver" in cases where the transfer penalty would endanger the applicant's health or other necessities of life. The states will have to develop these procedures in the near future.

Do I always have to pay a penalty when I transfer assets to someone else?

Certain transfers are exempt from the transfer penalty. In fact, you can transfer assets to the following recipients without triggering a transfer penalty:

- Your spouse.
- Your blind or disabled child.
- Into a trust for someone under 65 and disabled.

In addition to the recipients above, you're allowed to transfer your home to the following people without penalty:

- Your child under the age of 21.
- Your child who has lived with you for at least two years and provided care for you while he or she was there.
- Your sibling who is a part owner of the home and has lived there at least one year.

Income Guidelines

The general rule under Medicaid is that you must pay all of your income to the nursing home with a couple of small exceptions. You can keep $60 a month for personal needs allowance, which includes expenses like toothpaste, shampoo, etc. You can deduct any uncovered medical expenses. These exceptions vary state by state.

If you're married, your healthy spouse's income doesn't count against your Medicaid eligibility. Your healthy spouse's income is usually not affected by nursing home costs either. However, if most of your income as a couple is in your name and you're going to a nursing home, that income must go to the nursing home.

But what if your healthy spouse doesn't have enough income to live on? In this situation, Medicaid will allow your healthy spouse to keep a portion of your income (as opposed to your assets). The amount is determined by a formula called the Minimum Monthly Maintenance Needs Allowance (MMMNA). The MMMNA currently ranges from about $1,500 to $2,400 a month. If your healthy spouse's income falls below the MMMNA, Medicaid will make up the difference between the spouse's income and the cost of the nursing care, and will allow your spouse to receive part of your income.

> **Example 1:** Married Couple MMMNA
> Ricky and Lucy have a joint income of $2,800 a month, $2,000 of which is in Ricky's name. When Ricky goes into a nursing home, he's eligible for Medicaid. But Lucy's monthly income is only $800 a month. Medicaid determines that Lucy's MMMNA is $2,100 a month. That means she is allowed to keep $1,300 of Ricky's monthly income with the remaining $700 of income going to the nursing home.

Some states, though not Massachusetts, require a contribution from the healthy spouse's income if it exceeds certain limits.

Estate Guidelines

State Medicaid has the right to seek reimbursement for nursing home costs from your estate. This is known as "estate recovery." If you're married, the estate recovery process can't take place until the death of your healthy spouse.

States must try to recover assets from your probate estate. However, states do have the option of seeking recovery against assets that pass outside of probate, such as those jointly held, those in trusts, or those in life estate, if they so choose. Because states usually try to recover assets from your probate estate, this may be an added reason to avoid probate.

> **Example 1:** Estate Recovery
> Carmine's $400,000 home is a non-countable asset for Medicaid eligibility. When he dies, the home is included as part of his probate estate and passes through a will to his brother Johnny. The state puts a claim against the home as reimbursement for the $150,000 Carmine's nursing home care cost the government over the years.

> *Massachusetts expanded estate recovery to include non-probate assets for Medicaid recipients who died after July 1, 2003. However, the Massachusetts legislature voted to delay implementation of this law, and then in late 2004 it was repealed[2]. This issue is in flux and should be monitored for future attempts to expand estate recovery.*

---

[2] Massachusetts General Laws Chapter 118E Section 31.

Property Guidelines

If you're a Medicaid recipient and you keep your home while you're away at a nursing home, the state places a lien on the property. This means that the state has to be notified and paid back from the proceeds of the sale if the property is sold while you're still alive. The lien is removed upon your death.

The state doesn't always place a lien on your property when you become eligible for Medicaid. There are exceptions. For example, no lien will be placed upon your property if your spouse or minor/disabled child is using it as a primary residence.

LONG-TERM VS. CRISIS PLANNING (WHY IT'S BETTER TO PLAN AHEAD)

As we noted before, nursing home care typically costs between $40,000 and $100,000 a year depending on location and level of care. Failing to plan properly for these costs might force you to spend down your savings until you qualify for Medicaid, which leaves very little of your hard-earned money for loved ones in your bloodline.

When it comes to planning for the future, it's always better to plan ahead, but life sometimes throws unexpected curveballs your way, and you can't always be prepared for things as much as you want. In these crisis situations when you find yourself faced with sudden illness or incapacitated by accident, there are always short-term planning options you can turn to as a last resort.

Long -Term Planning Techniques
(When You Have Time to Plan For Medicaid)

Long-term planning provides the best opportunity to protect assets for Medicaid. There are several techniques you can use:

You can give away your assets

Medicaid has a 60 month (five year) look-back period beyond which you can transfer assets to family and loved ones without incurring a penalty. Therefore, transfers made more than five years before you apply for Medicaid won't hurt you in terms of eligibility. The downside to this technique, of course, is that you no longer own assets and won't be able to receive income generated by them.

You can protect assets in a trust

Trusts are holding-boxes that allow you to shelter, manage, and invest assets while you're alive and long after you're dead.

The tax advantages created by trusts were discussed in Chapter 9, but certain trusts offer additional benefits for long-term care planning. Some trusts are better at helping you qualify for Medicaid than others. You should take this into account before you have a lawyer create one for you.

A revocable or living trust:

A revocable or living trust does not protect assets for Medicaid purposes. Assets placed in these kinds of trusts are countable because you reserve the right to take these assets back any time you want. Medicaid therefore considers assets placed in a living trust to be available for long-term care.

Irrevocable trust:

An irrevocable trust offers a certain amount of asset protection for Medicaid purposes. If the irrevocable trust is created as "income only" (meaning that you only get income from the trust and have no access to principal) the principal isn't counted against you for Medicaid eligibility. Any income received from the trust must be paid to the nursing home once you become a resident. You may not be able to keep much for yourself, but at least you'll be able to protect the trust principal for your bloodline.

Keep in mind that transfers to an irrevocable trust, like all other transfers, have a five year look-back period. Also keep in mind that irrevocable trusts, as a whole, are inflexible and can't be changed. Once you put principal into the trust, you lose access to it for good.

The testamentary trust:

A testamentary trust also offers some asset protection as far as Medicaid eligibility goes. As we noted before, this type of trust is created as part of your will. It doesn't take effect until the will passes through probate.

There's a special rule under Medicaid that allows you to set up a testamentary trust for your nursing home spouse without disqualifying him or her for Medicaid, as long as trust payments are made to the spouse at the discretion of the trustee. In this situation, trust assets can be used to pay for services not covered by Medicaid.

You can protect your home with a life estate

A life estate allows you to retain the use of your home for life while directing the remainder to pass to someone else when you die. By changing the title of your home into a life estate you allow it to pass directly to your children (or another beneficiary of your choice) without going through probate and without having to pay estate recovery charges. Of course, this is only useful in states that limit their claims to property in your probate estate for repayment of Medicaid costs. Life estate property is still subject to the five year look-back period for Medicaid eligibility and the $500,000 home equity limit.

You can purchase long-term care insurance

Long-term care insurance covers nursing home costs for a limited period of time (e.g., 24 months) and for a certain amount per month (e.g., $4,500). It enables you in the short-term to avoid having to go on Medicaid.

There are two factors that will help you decide whether or not to purchase long-term care insurance. One factor is cost (long-term care insurance can be expensive). The other factor is insurability (some companies won't sell it to you if you have certain pre-existing medical conditions).

If you decide to purchase long-term care insurance, make sure the policy has enough coverage and that it's adjusted for inflation. Also make sure that the coverage lasts at least five years (the look back period for Medicaid).

> *You should check with your employer or your insurance agent for long-term care options.*

Crisis Planning Techniques: What to Do if You Don't Have Time

There are situations when you don't have enough time to plan for nursing home care. In these crisis situations caused by sudden illness or accident, there are two main techniques you can use to protect assets for Medicaid eligibility.

Reverse Mortgages

A reverse mortgage allows you to turn your home equity into cash. It is a loan against your home that you do not have to pay back until you die or sell the home. You can receive the money as a lump sum, credit line, monthly payments, or a combination thereof. You must own your home and be 62 or older to qualify. The proceeds from a reverse mortgage can be used to help pay for your nursing home costs and qualify for Medicaid.

Example 1: Reverse Mortgage and the "Valuable House"
Frank owns a $710,000 home outright and lives in a state
where the average nursing home costs $7,000 a month.
One day he has a stroke and is forced into a nursing home.
His house is $210,000 above the $500,000 home equity
limit to qualify for Medicaid. Before he goes, he takes out
a $210,000 reverse mortgage, which he can use to pay for
his nursing home care for up to 30 months (30 months x
$7,000/month = $210,000). After he spends the $210,000
on his nursing home care, he can apply for Medicaid, since
his home equity is now reduced to $500,000 ($710,000 –
$210,000 = $500,000). By using a reverse mortgage, Frank
was able to qualify for Medicaid and prevent his home
equity from counting against him.

You can convert countable assets into non-countable ones

You can protect your savings from nursing home costs by purchasing non-countable assets with countable assets (stocks, bonds,
and cash). These are the non-countable assets you can buy:

- **A home:** You can buy a home, pay off a mortgage, or make
  repairs to an existing home with your countable assets. Just
  be aware of the $500,000 limit on home equity to qualify for
  Medicaid.

- **An automobile:** You can spend up to $4,500 on an automo-
  bile. Your healthy spouse can purchase an automobile for any
  amount.

- **A prepaid funeral:** You can use countable assets to pay for funeral expenses in advance of death.

- **An annuity:** Transferring assets that count against your Medicaid eligibility into an annuity could help you qualify for Medicaid without having to spend them down on nursing home costs. Recall that the limit for "countable" assets (most savings, investments, and real estate except for your home) is $2,000 for an individual and $99,540 (in 2006) for a married couple. Any excess over these amounts has to be spent down and is also subject to the five year "look back" and transfer penalty. However, most states don't consider the purchase of an annuity as a transfer that affects Medicaid eligibility. For the annuity to be exempt from the asset transfer penalty, it has to meet the following requirements: the annuity must be irrevocable, you (or your spouse) can't have rights to withdraw funds from the annuity other than the monthly payments, and the state must be named as a remainder beneficiary for the amount of nursing home assistance provided. Annuities can help you qualify for Medicaid in a pinch whether you are married or single.

  Example 1: The Married Couple
  Archie and Edith have countable assets worth $220,000. When Archie enters the nursing home, Edith is allowed to keep $99,540 (the maximum resource allowance for a spouse in 2006). She has to spend down the remaining $120,460 on Archie's care to qualify for Medicaid. If she takes the remaining $120,460 and purchases an annuity that will pay her $1,400 a month for a term not exceeding her life expectancy, she won't have to spend down the remaining assets. Archie will qualify immediately for Medicaid, and the annuity will provide Edith with income for the rest of her life.

Example 2: The Single Person

Nancy is single and has countable assets worth $125,000. As a single person, she would have to spend down to $2,000 to qualify for Medicaid when she enters a nursing home. However, if Nancy takes the $125,000 and purchases an annuity that will pay her $1,500 a month for a term not exceeding her life expectancy, she will become eligible for Medicaid since the annuity is not a countable asset. Nancy will still have to contribute her $1,500/month annuity income (and any other income) towards her nursing home care. The state has the right to get reimbursed for the money spent on Nancy's care (beyond her own contributions) when she dies. However, Medicaid usually pays less than the nursing home's private monthly rate, which means their cost recovery will be less than if Nancy had to pay the nursing home herself (without qualifying for Medicaid). By qualifying for Medicaid with the annuity and taking advantage of the lower Medicaid monthly nursing home rate, Nancy can preserve more for her family.

The Deficit Reduction Act of 2005 contains complicated and in some cases conflicting provisions with regard to annuities that will have to be worked out in the near future. These uncertainties should be unraveled as the states begin to implement the new law, so it is extremely important to seek professional guidance when making planning decisions in this area.

As you can see, long-term care and nursing home planning are complex and rapidly changing areas. It's extremely important to consult a qualified professional in order to preserve all that you can for your loved ones.

Conclusion

We hope you have enjoyed reading and learning from *No Blood, No Money*. You've worked hard for your money, so keeping it safe for yourself and your loved ones is very important. The information in this book is designed to help you do just that. There are so many things you can do to protect your money, from creating a thorough and detailed will to putting aside funds in savings accounts and trusts, that it is not hard to make sure your money goes where you want — it just takes knowledge and foresight. This book is a reminder of how essential effective estate planning is.

It is important to remember, however, that the financial and legal considerations of the issues addressed in the book are numerous. Once you've determined your wishes and needs, please consult your friendly neighborhood financial planner and/or lawyer so s/he can help you with your planning. This is such an important and complex area that we urge you to consult with a professional in order to protect your hard-earned money as much as possible.

Remember — no blood, no money!

Glossary

401(k): Retirement savings plans that you contribute to through your employer. Plans through non-profit employers are called **403(b)**.

Ademption: If you no longer own an item you have willed to someone at the time the will gets executed, the chosen beneficiary gets nothing.

Alternate Valuation Date: For estate tax purposes, you have the option of valuing the deceased's property on the date of death, or six months after the date of death if you expect the value to change in your favor during that time.

Annuity: A contract with an insurance company to receive periodic payments (income) for life or a term of years. The payments can be fixed or variable depending on the provisions in the contract. Certain annuities protect your principal with a guaranteed minimum rate of interest.

Appreciation: An increase in value of a given object or investment.

Attachment: A legal proceeding to take and hold property to pay off a debt or judgment against you.

Beneficiaries: The people you want to inherit or receive your property; anyone who receives distributions of money or other assets from a trust. Individuals, charities, corporations, and government entities can be named as beneficiaries of a trust.

Bequests: These are gifts made to beneficiaries, usually in a will.

Bonds: A written promise by a borrower to pay interest periodically and repay the principal when the bond matures. Bonds are typically offered by government agencies (e.g., savings bonds) or corporations.

Capital Gains: Profits earned from the sale of investments. These include sale of stocks, bonds, mutual funds, or houses.

Capital Gains Tax: A tax on capital gains.

Certificates of Deposit (CDs): An investment account where you agree to leave money with the bank for a specific period of time without withdrawing it, in return for a specified rate of interest.

Codicil: An amendment to a will.

Condos: A form of real estate where individual units are owned separately and the property's common areas (parking lot, yard, pool, etc.) are owned jointly by all of the unit owners.

Co-op: A form of real estate where you buy shares of stock in a corporation that owns a building that is subdivided into individual units.

Dividends: Distribution of profits to stockholders in a corporation.

Durable Power of Attorney: Allows you to designate someone to manage and distribute assets during your life in case you're unable to do so because you are incompetent or incapacitated through illness.

Depreciation: A decrease in value of a given object or investment.

Estate Tax: A tax based on the value of total property you own at the time of your death, which is paid from the value of the estate itself, before the assets and property are transferred to the beneficiaries.

Estate Tax Credit: The value of assets you can pass on to family and friends after your death without paying any estate taxes.

Executor: The person you choose to manage the distribution of your property when you die according to instructions you give in your will; the manager of your estate.

Federal Deposit Insurance Corporation (FDIC): A government agency that insures bank accounts.

Fiduciary Bond: Security posted to a probate court by an executor of an estate in order to protect the estate's assets for the beneficiaries.

Fixed Index Annuity (FIA): An investment in an annuity whose returns are calculated based on growth in a particular index such as the S&P 500.

Gift Tax: A tax you pay when you transfer assets (e.g., property, money, stocks, bonds, jewelry) to someone else during your lifetime.

Gift Tax Credit: The amount of money or other property you're allowed to give away to others during your lifetime without owing a tax on the transfer.

Generation Skipping Tax (GST): A tax on assets over $1 million transferred over two generations (e.g., from grandparent to grandchild).

Inheritance Tax: A tax on inheritances, which is drawn directly from the beneficiary.

Intangible Property: Property that lacks a concrete, physical substance, but has a symbolic value — a dollar bill, a share of stock, or a bond.

Intestate: Dying without a will

IRA — Individual Retirement Account: A personal retirement investment that allows an individual to contribute certain sums annually and receive special tax allowances. There are two types of IRA's: Traditional IRA and Roth IRA.

Laws of Intestacy: If you don't have a will at the time of your death, these laws determine who will receive your property and the amount each living beneficiary is entitled to receive.

Legal Residence: The location of your home — town, county, and state of residence.

Life Estate: A type of ownership of real estate often used to avoid probate: ownership of the real estate terminates on the death of the owner and transfers directly to a named beneficiary on the deed.

Medicare: A federal program that provides health coverage for seniors (citizens over 65).

Medicaid: A joint federal/state program that provides medical assistance to children, seniors, and disabled persons who meet income and asset requirements. It's a means-tested program limited only to those with financial need, often used for nursing home costs.

Mutual Funds: Accounts in which investors pool their money together to buy stocks, bonds, or other types of investments.

Net Asset Value: The sum total of all assets in a fund divided by the number of shares in the fund.

Prenuptial Agreement: A legally biding agreement made prior to marriage that determines property ownership rights during and after marriage.

Principal: The amount you invest in a given asset or security.

Pour-Over Will: Provision in a will that distributes assets to a trust — the money will "pour over" into the trust.

Probate: A legal proceeding conducted by a state court that oversees and manages the distribution of your property after you die in order to clear title of ownership on your property, so that it can pass from you to your beneficiaries as dictated by your will or by the laws of intestacy, if you don't have a will.

Settlor: Person creating a trust.

Situs: The location of your trust; the state designated as the home of your trust.

Social Security: A federal program established in the 1930s to provide retirement and disability benefits. Funded through payroll tax on employees and employers.

Stocks: Shares of ownership in a company.

Tangible Property: Anything you can touch: jewelry, furniture, cars, antiques, stamps, art, household goods, baseball cards, etc.

Testator: The person writing a will.

Trusts: A kind of holding-box that invests and distributes your assets for you and your beneficiaries; a legal entity that holds and manages your assets while you're alive or after you're dead. Often used to avoid probate.

Trustees: Individuals (friends or family members) or corporate fiduciaries (e.g., banks or trust companies) who manage your trust.

Trust Document: The agreement of trust.

Vesting: A 401(k) provision that requires you to work with your employer for a minimum number of years before you are able to withdraw your employer's contributions.

Will: A legal document that communicates your desires and intentions for the distribution of your property at your death. Can be revoked or amended during your lifetime.

About the Authors

Richard L. Rubino, JD

Richard L. Rubino is a managing partner of Rubino & Liang, LLC, a full services firm located in Newton, MA. He is a member of the National Academy of Elder Law Attorneys and the Boston Estate Planning Council. He is a seven-time recipient of the Top of the Table Award, given by the Million Dollar Roundtable in recognition for great achievement within the financial services industry. Rich has also been named by the "Who's Who" registry as a member of the elite "Who's Who in Business Worldwide."

Rich was born and raised in Brooklyn, New York and settled in Brookline, Massachusetts after attending law school and volunteering for a year with Volunteers in Service to America (VISTA). He received his Juris Doctor (JD) degree from Suffolk University in 1969, and is a member of the Massachusetts, New York, and Florida Bar Associations. He advises his clients on legal matters and works with other attorneys who specialize in different fields of law. He and his wife, Winnie, have two children, Jamie and Ryan.

Samuel J. Liang

Samuel Liang is a managing partner at Rubino & Liang, LLC, a financial services firm located in Newton, MA. Some of Sam's past achievements include being the recipient of the 1999 Boston Business Journal's 40 Under 40 award. In 2000 he also received the prestigious Francis Lowell Cabot Award as the Alumni of the year for the University of Massachusetts-Lowell. He is a nine-time recipient of the Top of the Table Award, given by the Million Dollar Roundtable in recognition for great achievement within the financial services industry. Sam has also been named by the "Who's Who" registry as a member of the elite "Who's Who in Business Worldwide."

Born in Hong Kong, Sam came to this country in 1974. When he arrived he couldn't speak English. By the time he graduated high school, he ranked in the top 10% of his class. Sam and his wife Eileen live in Bedford with their four children, Devin, Samantha, Ethan, and Harrison.

Along with his partner Richard Rubino, Sam Liang co-hosts "Senior Financial Focus," the Boston area syndicated financial talk show for seniors heard throughout Eastern Massachusetts every Sunday morning 9 a.m. to 10 a.m. on WRKO (680 AM).

Rubino & Liang, LLC

Rubino & Liang, LLC is a financial services firm that provides advice, products, and services primarily to retirement-aged clients in the Greater Boston area. From retirement and estate planning to wealth transfer and preservation strategies, the firm is highly focused on the needs of the pre-retirement and retired individual.

Rubino & Liang's innovative approach has earned its founders industry recognition as leaders in catering to the needs of the retired individual. Founders Richard Rubino, JD and Samuel Liang also host a successful radio talk show that provides seniors with information and insights into the unique financial challenges that face the retired individual.

With their clients they emphasize:

- Sound basic principles and common sense
- Principal-protected accounts when appropriate
- Asset allocations that have growth with emphasis on safety
- Employing tax efficiency and/or tax deferral strategies
- Protecting real estate and family heirlooms
- Using trusts when appropriate for smooth transition to heirs
- Reducing and/or eliminating probate and estate taxes
- Protecting and preserving assets if nursing home is needed

"My parents lived through the Depression, worked overtime to put me and my sisters through college, and uprooted their lives to move to America from Hong Kong so we could have a chance at a better life," says Sam. He often thinks about this, which drives him and gives him the passion to ensure a level of comfort for his parents during their retirement and the same dedication to all of his clients.

SERVICES OFFERED

As members of the National Academy of Elder Law Attorneys (NAELA) and members of the Boston Estate Planning Council (BEPC), Rich and Sam stay informed and current on any changes in the law. They specialize in asset preservation strategies for seniors over 50 years old.

- Investment recommendations for pre-retirees and post-retirees.
- Estate planning from basic wills to trust design.
- Asset protection for business owners to nursing home disasters.
- Inheritance planning and use of the "No Blood, No Money" technique.

There is a lot of information out there to choose from. Call us to help you choose the best strategies for you at 877-630-8787.